SHINGAS

THE BATTLE OF THE IROQUOIS PEOPLE
AGAINST THE ENGLISH RED COATS

EK-2 PUBLISHING

Your Satisfaction Is Our Goal!

Dear Readers,

First, we would like to thank you for purchasing this book. Our goal is to inspire readers from all over the world with our historical and military novels and biographies.

We are a family business, and our team thrives to offer you a unique reading experience and of course, we want to increase our quality with each book published.

We are grateful for your feedback as well as ideas about books you may want to read in the future. Your opinion matters to us. Do you have any comments or criticism? Please let us know. Your feedback is of great value to us and of course to our authors as well. Be part of our publishing journey and our EK-2 publishing family. Write to us at:

info@ek2-publishing.com

And now we wish you an entertaining reading experience with this book.

Your EK-2 Publishing Team

For Elisabeth

PROLOGUE

The war was over. The bitter struggle, which had seen the two great European nations of France and England locked in a bloody conflict for seven years had finally ended, and together with all her dependencies Canada now had a new ruler, King George the Third of England. Now all that remained to be done was for the victor to take possession of those western forts and outposts which remained in French hands, and it is there that our story begins.

Located on the western bank of the river whose name it bore, with a hundred or so small houses and a well-built barracks enclosed within its high palisaded walls, Fort Detroit was more like a fortified town than a military outpost. Formed in the shape of a square with a wooden bastion at each corner, all armed with a cannon, and its gated entrance guarded by a blockhouse its Canadian inhabitants had little to fear from attacks by warring savages. And while not impregnable against a more resolute force, with its large garrison of French soldiers, it was an impressive stronghold, nevertheless. Sadly, on a chilly November day in 1760, none of this would matter, and without a single shot being fired its capitulation was secured by a single sheet of paper.

CHAPTER ONE

From the quadrangle of firmed earth surrounded on each side by weathered palisades, Captain Beletre, the garrison commander, a stout, middle-aged man, immaculately dressed in a three-quarter length grey jacket with deep cuffs of dark blue, worn over a blue waistcoat embellished with gold buttons, fixed his doleful gaze on the flag billowing in the stiffening breeze. His aristocratic features, marred somewhat by a large aquiline nose, fixed in a grim expression. He had resolved to defend his post but when handed a copy of the capitulation by the English officer, together with a letter from the Marquis de Vaundreuil directing that the post should be given up without resistance, he had no choice but to surrender.

In the fort's eastern bastion, bathed in a mellow light as a shaft of sunlight pierced the cloud-filled November sky a lone French soldier stepped forward and greeted by a rousing cheer from the detachment of English soldiers watching from outside the walls, untying the rope at the foot of the flagstaff he began lowering the Fleur De Lis. Unable to watch, Beletre lowered his gaze. As a soldier, he felt the bitterness of defeat and as a Frenchman, he felt the sadness of an empire lost. But as a husband and a father, he was glad it was over. Glad that he was done with war. For him, the moment of certainty had come two years earlier at Ticonderoga, when even as they perished in their hundreds on the French breastworks in a tempest of musket-balls, the heroism and determined valor displayed that day by the English soldiers showed a desire to wrest this land from whoever laid claim to it that was unstoppable. Pushing the bitter memory from his mind, he turned to the warrior standing beside him, a Seneca war chief and ally of the French, and offered him a benign smile.

The Indian stared back at him with ink-black eyes. He was tall for his race, his body lean and muscular, his savage features emblazoned with war paint. A single white heron's feather adorned his scalp-lock, and suspended around his neck was a bear claw necklace. His only clothing was a breechcloth and thigh-length leather leggings tied at the knee. Hanging down from his belt were a knife and a tomahawk. When he spoke, his French was imbued with the eloquence of his native tongue and although the language was foreign to him, learned over many hours from black-robed Jesuits, his mastery of it was commendable.

"Why do you lay down your arms when we are many and they are few?"

"You think I don't want to fight?" Beletre replied, his face flushed with anger, his words imbued with bitterness. "But I am forbidden. In France our Great Father has fallen asleep and while he slumbers, he desires that we make peace with the English."

"And what is to become of us your brothers? Must we also make peace with these English dogs?"

"I must obey the wishes of my King, and you must obey them also."

"He is not my King."

"That may be so, but Shingas must know he cannot fight the English alone."

"Shingas fought the Yengeese before his French brothers took up arms against them. Shingas took many scalps and soon he will take many more."

Overcome by a sense of sadness at Shingas' words and aware of the fate he knew awaited him and his people, Beletre paused for a moment, struggling to think of a way of conveying to this savage warrior the complex web of politics and intrigue that had led to this moment. But he knew it was hopeless. It would be easier to make the length of rope out of sand. So instead, adopting a more conciliatory tone, he lied.

"Shingas is a great warrior, but he must be patient, soon the Great Father will awaken and then he will send his armies to drive the English from the lands of his children."

"The English King does not sleep and if Shingas does not fight, these dogs dressed in red will devour my people."

Resigned to the hopelessness of further reasoning, touching a hand to his black, gold-trimmed tricorne hat, Beletre turned and walked away, contenting himself as he strode across the small quadrangle with thoughts of a return to the house, he loved on the Rue St Antoine in Paris and a reunion with a family he had not seen for over five years. With both of his daughters now married, there was also the possibility of grandchildren to enjoy in his old age. But first, there was the formality of surrender to attend to. Ahead of him, flanked by English soldiers the French garrison, disarmed and dejected filed out through the gates and made their way along the narrow dirt road leading down to the river, and the small flotilla of whale boats waiting to transport them across the stormy waters of Lake Eire into captivity.

Watching from their village on the opposite bank a large crowd of Pottawattamie and Wyandot warriors dressed in painted shirts and fluttering headdresses, faithless allies of the French looked on with amazement. Their primitive minds were unable to understand why with so many soldiers the French had surrendered so easily to an enemy so few in number. With a gesture, Shingas gathered his war party around him. Robbed of their muskets and powerless to change the unfolding events, falling in behind the grey-coated Troupes De La Marine, they left the sanctuary of the fort.

Off to one side where the rising ground formed a low hill, robbed of the battle he was so looking forward to Lieutenant Brehm observed proceedings with a mounting sense of disappointment. That was until he caught sight of Shingas and his warriors at the rear of the column. Turning to where a company of Roger's Rangers, their russet green uniforms in stark contrast to that worn by their enemy were taking their ease, he gestured to them urgently. Obediently, carrying their muskets at the port, like a pack of hounds called to heel the soldiers jogged towards him. Mindful that as prisoners of war the French soldiers were to be afforded a degree of respect the young officer was equally aware that the same degree of latitude did not apply to their heathen allies. Buoyed up by the thought he began striding away down the sloping ground towards the dirt road. The company of Rangers quickly formed up into two columns behind him. Alerted by the flurry of activity as the English soldiers gathered around the young officer, Shingas watched with mounting trepidation as they began making their way towards the road. Something about the officer's purposeful stride worried him. But what concerned him more was that unlike the remainder of the company, the two soldiers bringing up the rear both had their muskets slung over their shoulders and they were carrying manacles and leg irons. With a guttural cry, Shingas called out a warning and leaving the dirt road, he began running towards the cleared ground in front of the fort. A killing field for any attacker's foolhardy enough venture upon it. Heeding Shingas' warning, to a man the war party followed after him. Leaping over the stumps of the decapitated trees with the grace and agility of deer, their hearts pounding as they raced towards the safety of the forest.

Reaching the road, the company of Rangers quickly formed up into two ranks. The front rank dropping down onto one knee while the second rank formed up a pace behind them. Pausing for a moment to give each man time to raise his musket and select his target, the young officer cried out. "Fire!"
The sound of exploding muskets shattered the silence. The volley of musket balls droning like angry bees as they flew among the fleeing war party. Instantly, six of the warriors tumbled to the ground, a bloody hole in their back. Spurred on, Shingas and the survivors raced headlong for the sanctuary of the trees. Behind them, with practiced precision, the soldiers reloaded their muskets. Ramming wadding and ball home with their rods before priming the musket pan with powder. When all were ready, their lieutenant called out. "Present! Fire!"

Once more the deafening crash of musket fire shattered the silence and just yards from the safety of the tree line the three warriors lagging behind the others, were struck by the hail of lead balls. Tumbling to the ground like skittles struck by a well-thrown cheese. With his youthful cheeks flushed with color, Lieutenant Brehm ordered his men to fix bayonets. Then, pistol in hand, striding forward as though he were marching across a parade-ground he made his way across the uneven ground towards the fallen Indians. Behind him, the naked steel of their bayonets glinting in the late morning sun, the soldiers formed up into a single line and advanced across the cleared ground, their boots sinking into the

10

soft mould. Reaching the fallen Indians, regardless of whether they were dead or alive moving from body to body the Rangers began stabbing them with their pig-sticker bayonets as though they were just lumps of meat. Then, with their murderous work completed, their once gleaming bayonets dripping with blood, led by the jubilant young officer they made their way back to the road.

Concealed by the dense foliage his face devoid of expression, Shingas watched their butchery. Taught from childhood to conceal all emotions, the lesson would not leave him but in his heart, he swore he would have his revenge. With a last look towards the fort with the blood-red flag of Saint George flying above its ramparts he turned and with his war party gathered around him, Shingas moved away into the safety of the darkening forest.

CHAPTER TWO

With its only window covered by a wooden shutter, the room was cloaked in darkness. What little light there was, came in through the partially opened door. Standing beside it, his ear pressed against the opening straining to catch the sounds coming from the adjoining room; a man's voice but so quiet he could barely hear it, was a tall well-built man in his mid-twenties. His handsome features are framed by a mane of dark brown shoulder-length hair. The muscular contours of his naked chest standing out in a relief-like torso of a Greek statue.

Oblong in shape the adjoining room was sparsely furnished. Serving as both kitchen and living room with a curtained area in the far corner, concealing a small bed. A ten-foot-long table-board set on trestles, and surrounded by six chairs dominated the centre of the room. With a solid oak door secured by two metal bolts set in the far wall. Flanked on each side by a narrow window, each covered by a wooden shutter. A stone fireplace housing a large cast-iron stove occupied much of the longest wall. It's dying fire bathing the room in a soft orange glow. Seated at either end of the table were two people, their faces illuminated by the light from a glass-sided lantern suspended above them from a roof beam. The silence was only broken by the rhythmic ticking of a brass-crowned clock, resting on the mantelshelf above the fireplace.

Samuel Endicote, a broad-shouldered man in his sixties with a weathered face and close-cropped greying hair looked across at the woman facing him. His small, bright eyes staring into her face, expectantly. Holding his gaze for a moment Esther lowered her eyes, focusing them on Samuel's calloused hands, a farmer's hands, placed palms down on the table in front of him. Unexpected as they were his words had unsettled her. Leaving her thoughts flitting between doubts and possibilities. Overshadowing both was a sense of disbelief. Could he really wish this of her? When he spoke again, the sound of his voice, although not loud, startled her.

"Well, have you no answer for me?"

Sensing the impatience in his tone, Esther waited a moment longer before replying.

"You. . . You wish me to marry Adam?"

"Yes, and in exchange, you shall have your freedom and more besides."

Esther felt her heartbeat quicken. Could this be possible? A simple *yes*, and she would be free of her indenture? But before she could utter the word, others spilt uninvited from her mouth.

"But Adam is . . .He is . . ."

"A child! A simpleton!" said Samuel spitting out the words as though they were bile.

Annoyed at her stupid outburst Esther averted her eyes.

Clenching his fists, Samuel leaned forward, his lips curled into a salacious grin.

"That he may be but for all that he is, he is still a man."

Shocked by the implication, Esther lifted a hand to her mouth.

Pleased with the response his words had evoked Samuel glared at her for a moment before settling back in his chair. Allowing his anger to dissipate before continuing in a softer tone.

"But that is not the reason for what I propose", said Samuel, pausing for a moment as if to gather his thoughts. "When I am gone our first-born Adam will inherit this farm but how long do you suppose before his brother Saul steals it away from him? Answer me that."

Her composure restored, sensing he had more to say Esther remained silent.

"Oh, I know my sons well, and Saul would do it of that I have no doubt. But I have also come to know you mistress Colwill, and it is my belief that if you were Adam's wife then he'd surely not succeed."

Meeting his gaze, surer now of her position and in the possibilities the matter at hand offered her Esther remained silent, waiting for his impatience to get the better of him.

"So, what do you say? Will you do it? Will, you wed Adam?" Samuel spoke while striking the table with the palm of his hand.

"And I should be freed of my indenture?" Esther replied calmly.

"Indeed." said Samuel, sensing her possible agreement. "I may only be a farmer, but I cannot have a son of mine wedded to a servant." The smallest smile softened his features.

"And be mistress in my own right?"

"You have my word on it."

Although her mind was already made up, Esther paused for a moment before giving him her reply. It would do no harm to let him wait.

"Then I will agree to it ", she said confidently. "I will do what you ask."

Pushing the door shut Saul turned away. Although he had heard everything that was said, rather than being angry, it was a smile that lit his face. With practiced ease, he padded across the darkened room and down the aisle between the two narrow cots. Pausing for a moment he gazed down at the recumbent figure of Kit his youngest brother, his head buried in a pillow, lost in sleep. The boy's hand clutched a corner of the blanket as though fearful that someone would snatch it away from him. Reassured by the heavy breathing coming from his other two brothers who shared the bed opposite that neither of them was aware of his eavesdropping, Saul lowered himself onto his bed. Although he was tired, the prospect of something other than sleep was more than enough to keep him awake.

In the silence, the sound of the mantel clock striking midnight was like the clanging of a steeple bell in Saul's ears. Taking care not to disturb Kit, he climbed off the bed and navigated his way to the door. Carefully lifting the wooden latch, he stepped silently into the adjoining room. With the faint glow emanating from the stove and the sallow light of a single candle giving substance to the table and chairs, barefooted and wearing nothing except a pair of home-spun breeches soundlessly, Saul crossed to the curtain suspended on hooks from the ceiling. Grasping at one end he pulled it aside, revealing a narrow bed pushed up against the wall. Lying on it, her body covered by a patterned quilt, Esther gazed up at him. Her grey-blue eyes glistening like jewels in the guttering candlelight. She was not surprised to see him. She had known he would come. Just as surely as she knew he would have been listening to all that was said between her and his father. Pushing herself upright, with an inviting smile she pulled aside the blanket, revealing herself to him. The simple cotton nightdress she was wearing opened at the neck, exposing the soft valley between her breasts. Stepping closer Saul gazed down at her, desire welling up inside him like lava. Smiling seductively, reaching down Esther slowly pulled the hem of her nightgown up over her thighs. Devouring her with his eyes, with trembling fingers Saul untied the leather strap around his waist, letting his breeches fall around his ankles.

Staring up at his naked body, reaching out her hand Esther pulled him down onto the bed beside her. With his throat dry with passion, gripping her shoulders in a vice-like grip Saul pushed her down onto the bed. Arching her neck, Esther stared up at him her eyes smoldering, her lips full and inviting. With a half-suppressed cry, Saul covered her with his mouth. His lips crushing hers. Moaning softly, Esther wrapped her arms around him. Pulling him into her, his naked chest crushing her breasts. Freeing his arm Saul reached his hand down between her thighs, forcing them apart. His finger searching for her womanhood in the silky triangle of pubic hair. His heart racing as he caressed the velvety softness of her secret wound.

Inflamed by his touch, groaning with pleasure Esther gripped his arm, and pulling his hand away she spread her legs, wrapping them tightly around him. Encircling his waist with her naked thighs and pulling him into her. With the cloying scent of her musk clogging his nostrils, consumed with lust, Saul plunged into her. Feeling her body arching as he thrust into her again, and again, in an ever-quickening rhythm. Her wide child-bearing hips pushing upwards, meeting his thrusts with her own. Her nails clawing his naked back, digging into his skin like talons. In moments it was over, and spent, Saul rolled off her. His chest heaving, his body glistening with sweat. With a pretense at modesty, pulling down her nightdress Esther turned onto her side. Propping herself up on her elbow she stared into his handsome face, her gaze washing over his features, his dark liquid eyes, the perfect line of his jaw. She knew there was no love between them. Just an unspoken need. A hunger for each other's bodies. But for all that their illicit lovemaking suited them both. Satisfying his manly needs while giving her moments of pleasure in a life filled with drudgery and hardships. Turning away from her lover, lying on her back Esther's thoughts returned to the momentous decision she had made the previous evening and its forthcoming consequences. The changes being married to Adam would bring to her life. A life free of servitude. The ever-present dread of being passed from family to family like a chattel gone forever. And it was at that moment that she experienced a feeling of utter contentment.

CHAPTER THREE

There were seven of them, each dressed in a greasy hunting frock of smoked deerskin fringed with horsehair. A rough and truculent bunch with stubble chins and lank, shoulder-length hair tucked under caps of varying styles. Some were cut from felt and stuck with feathers, others fashioned from the skin of beaver or otter. Hardy men brought together without a care for their compatibility. It was enough that each of them hated work as much as they did Indians, and who were willing to suffer a little of both for the pure perils of the life and its fickle rewards.

Two weeks earlier five of them had left the frontier city of Albany with its busy wharves, and narrow streets crowded with families seeking a new life in the vast wilderness beyond. In a hired bateau, crewed by men with a knowledge of the river, heavily loaded with every possible artefact of trade including six-quarter barrels of raw whiskey, they had rowed up the Mohawk. A noisy, singing crew until the effort required for pulling on the heavy oars had taken all their breath. On passed the old Dutchman's town of Schenectady with its pretty timber houses and waving children. Then around the long bend in the river to Fort Hunter standing boldly at the mouth of the Schoharie. With a hello, to the sentries, as they passed beneath the tall ramparts, bending their backs by early evening they reached Fort Herkimer at the German flats and the welcoming prospect of board and lodgings for the night.

Dawn saw them on their way once more, and after a wearying pull against a current which had caught the scent of the sea, they reached Fort Stanwix at the head of the river navigation. Here the bateau was unloaded and the goods put inside the walls for the night and for men who were used to a less arduous life, supper and a welcome bed. Early next morning with the bateau sent back down river, the trade goods were loaded onto the backs of sixteen packhorses. All except for the ten muskets, which despite the trader's protests were confiscated by the fort's commander who feared they might be used by the capricious savages against his majesty's subjects. Passing out through the gates they began their journey westward, and by mid-morning, after almost losing two of their animals while fording Wood Creek, a wild, rushing stream bordered by towering elms and ageless oaks they entered the dark recesses of the forest. The serried ranks of towering pines, their scaly trunks piercing the sky crowding around them like an impenetrable barrier. But they were on familiar ground now, and after twenty more hard miles, they reached the little wooden fortress of Royal Blockhouse and their journey's end.

Located at the eastern end of Oneida Lake, the fort had been abandoned many years ago by the military. Its leaky roof and crumbling walls, now the residence of an old Sutler provisioner and his two milk cows who made his living by trading with a village of Oneida Indians on the opposite shore. But it was not here that the packtrain, with its wealth of trade goods, was destined. Standing beside the decaying outpost, its door and windows looking out onto the lake was a rectangular building constructed of logs, with a sloping shingle roof. Almost twice the size of the fort, with a living space large enough to accommodate a dozen men the warehouse was owned by Thomas Gann. With little interest in its regal name, he had chosen the site for his trading post based purely on its location. A bold and forward-looking man, who at the end of the war with the French had turned his energies towards the profitable though often precarious business of fur trading. Rivalry among the various traders was fierce and murder was commonplace. But for all that, great profits rewarded the successful and Gann, whose character combined the astuteness of a banker with the morality of a highwayman, was not a man to be unsuccessful. And so it was, that thanks to his quick mind, and greedy fingers the seven men and their packhorses now found themselves venturing into the heart of the Genessee Valley, the home of the Seneca.

For three days they travelled through its primaeval forest with its scaly towers of bark, tangled thickets, and pine swamps, and although a June sun burned in the sky above, beneath the endless canopy all was shade and shadow. Only its warmth penetrated the verdure where among the pines, spruce and maple, it hung like an invisible mist, heavy with the pungent perfume of resin and decay. With day and night colliding they emerged from its gloomy depths and made their way along the margin of a narrow lake. Its surface was shimmering in the late afternoon sun as though it were covered by a million golden pennies. Weariness betrayed itself in the men's rugged faces and in the dull, dark eyes of the horses, so all were relieved when reaching a narrow beach, their leader a man named Quinty Soule called a halt. All around them, thickly wooded hills ran down to reflect upon the water but here lake and land met on a level. The forest held at bay by a narrow meadow of pale grass, flanked by white birch and alders.

Untying a sack from one of the horses, Flute, a short, stocky man in his forties with the ruddy complexion of a jovial innkeeper emptied the assortment of blackened pots and pans onto the ground. While unqualified for the role of cook his willingness to undertake the culinary duties was enough to secure him the job. The others, as much from laziness as anything else, were more than willing to accept the occasional bouts of diarrhea rather than take on the task themselves. Leaving Flute to organize his kitchen, with the remainder of the traders busy unloading the bundles of trade goods from the horses, Blessing, a bear of a man with short stocky legs, together with a lanky youth named Linnet, his smallpox scarred face framed by long straggly hair, made their way into the trees in search of firewood. With the last of the horses stripped of their packs, leading them by their halters Doublejohn, the party's horse-minder tethered them to a length of rope strung out between two birch trees. Seeing the animals settled, retrieving a gunny sack from among the pile of traded goods, he moved along the line feeding each horse in turn a handful of corn. As darkness descended like a veil Blessing and Linnet returned laden with firewood, and with the spark from a flint they soon had a fire lit. Its welcoming glow attracting the others to it like moths to a flame. Last to arrive was McCallum, a wiry-built man with narrow shoulders, a tartan cap, a nod to his ancestry pulled around his ears. Setting down the animal-skin bundle he was carrying, running his tongue salaciously over his thin lips, he pulled back the flaps to reveal a haunch of venison. Their evening meal. Skewering the joint on the rusty iron pole which he kept among his utensils for just such a purpose, resting it in the notched ends of the two sticks set on each side of the fire, Flute began basting the purple flesh in a glutinous substance resembling axle grease. Their appetites wetted, the traders edged closer to the fire, their gaze fixed on the haunch of venison spitting and sizzling in the flames embrace. But even as the seven men watched their supper cooking, other eyes were watching them.

The four Seneca warriors were well hidden by the dense branches of spruce, their copper-colored skin encouraging concealment. Naked except for a breechcloth and thigh-length leggings, their heads shaved except for a single lock of hair, at the crown. Each of them was armed with a flint-lock musket. All that afternoon, unseen by the traders, they had shadowed the packtrain as it progressed through the forest. Watching as it moved ever deeper into their hunting grounds.
"They are Yengeese English traders. We will speak with them."
The warrior's name was Pahotan. His words were softly spoken. As the leader of the small hunting party, he spoke with authority. The other warriors, all young men remained silent. With his decision made, pointing to one of the warriors Pahotan climbed to his feet, and together, the pair slipped away into the surrounding trees.

Doublejohn was the first to see them. After supper, he had taken the last two horses down to the lake to wash their legs while they stood in the shallows slaking their thirst. All of them had suffered cuts, and scratches from the thorn bushes and tangled undergrowth they had encountered as they journeyed through the wilderness. And although the wounds were not deep, he knew that unless they were cleaned, come next morning these bloody cuts would prove irresistible to the ever-present swarms of flies. The last to be washed, with her nostrils flared the young mare nervously tap-stepping away from him, her neat ears laid back. Pulling gently on the horse's halter rope Doublejohn quickly brought her under control. Talking to her as he splashed the cooling water over her legs. His voice soft and reassuring. Satisfied that the last of the blood had been washed from the mare's legs, turning his back on the lake Doublejohn began leading the two horses back towards the camp. And it was then that he saw them.

Even without war paint, they exuded an aura of menace, and although a look of concern clouded Doublejohn's face when he spoke his voice was calm. His accent was pure Cornish.

"Look to, we haz us zum company."

Instantly, the men seated around the fire began reaching for their muskets. Turning as one to face the supposed danger.

"Steady lads, I don't think they mean us any harm", said Soule, and placing his musket on the ground he climbed to his feet and began slowly walking towards where Pahotan and the young warrior stood motionless, midway between the forest and the camp. A distance calculated to show their boldness while also giving them a good chance to escape should these Yengeese prove unfriendly. With a deer-skin shirt worn over scarlet leggings, and his long greasy black hair tied back in a single braid Quinty Soule epitomized the breed of men called Coureurs de bois wood runners by the French. More Indian than white some would day. In his late thirties, his weathered features were scarred by a purple welt running from his eye socket to his jaw. A visual testament to the dangers of a trader's life. Watching from the camp, while none of the others could hear what was being said, to a man they heaved a sigh of relief when they saw Soule turn around and begin leading the two Indians back towards the fire. Calling out to them as he approached.

"We've had us a stroke of luck boys. These here are Seneca and come morning they say they will guide us to their village."

"Meat will burn if it's not eaten", shouted Flute, more concerned about his meal being spoiled than worrying over a pair of savages. Quickly heeding his words, after finding a place at the fire, with little regard for manners, each man was soon hacking at the joint with his knife. Stuffing the cuts of meat into their mouths until they overflowed at the corners like a burst sack.

As the last of the meat was carved from the bone, wiping a sleeve across his greasy mouth lifting the large, blackened kettle off the fire, and with an unerring aim Flute began pouring the scalding hot coffee into three large tin cups. Soule, as befitting his status as captain had one to himself, the remaining pair being passed from lip to lip until they were drained, and topped up again until the kettle was empty. With the conclusion of the meal greeted by a chorus of hearty belches, dipping their greasy fingers into a pocket, the traders, with the exception of Flute who for reasons best known to himself had an aversion to the habit, removed their pipe, and tobacco. Lighting them with a stick from the fire, in minutes the air was filled with clouds of sweet-scented smoke. A delight to the nostrils and a deterrent against the blood-sucking insects which plagued the water's edge. As the evening began drawing in, spreading a blanket on the ground Bailey, a thin-faced man with deep-set eyes, removed a set of dice from the bullet sack suspended around his neck. Never ones to shy away from a spot of gambling the other traders quickly gathered around him. Each man removing a handful of musket balls from their shot pouches to be used as wagers.

Sitting apart from the others Soule looked over his cup at the loose circle of players, his gaze lingering on the two Indians. Each had a tomahawk and a scalping knife hanging from their belt, the latter carried on a high-necked sheath decorated with colored quills. With a leather satchel and a powder-horn slung across their shoulders, the straps crisscrossing their chest. Before losing interest in the pair Soule focused his interest on their rifles. The fact that both were military flintlocks of the type issued by the English to their Indian allies should have proved reassuring. But knowing the capricious nature of the Indians, Soule put little faith in it. Past experiences had taught him that such alliances could change in the blink of an eye. It was also common knowledge that many Seneca warriors had fought on the side of the French. Nevertheless, the older warrior had assured him that his people would welcome the trade goods they carried, and he had no reason to doubt him. If the pair were up to mischief, they would find out soon enough. Both he and the men in his company were used to facing such dangers so he was not overly concerned. They had been in situations like this many times before and they still had their scalps.

Eventually, as the evening passed into night the game was abandoned, and finding a spot around the dying fire, with the ground as a bed, their bellies full of venison the traders were soon asleep. The sound of their snoring a testament to the rigors of the day. Unable to settle, throwing some wood on the fire Soule warmed his cup from the dregs left in the kettle. From the lake, lost now in inky blackness, the melancholy notes of a loon were snatched up by a wind going nowhere, and scattered among the treetops.

CHAPTER FOUR

As usual, Flute was the first to crawl out from under his blanket, with a kettle boiling before the others began crowding around his fire sniffing the air like a pack of hungry dogs. Their complaints about the lateness of the meal were answered by a few well-chosen expletives from the cook. Breakfast was what remained of the meat left over from supper, and a dozen oatmeal biscuits seasoned with berries, warming on a skillet over the fire. The contents of the meal washed down with cups of scalding coffee. The first to finish eating, freeing the horses of their hobbles Doublejohn led them into camp, and with everyone lending themselves to the task they were soon loaded with their heavy packs. The horse-minder moving from animal to animal checking their girth straps and ensuring that none were too tight or too slack. With the meal over and every last cake devoured, pouring the remains of the coffee onto the fire Flute began putting away his pots and pans into a greasy gunnysack. That done, opening the front of his breeches, member in hand he relieved himself on what remained of the fire. Extinguishing the last of its flames. Seeing that Doublejohn had finished fussing over his horses, eager to be on his way Soule shouted out.

"All's ready, let's be gone."

Alerted by his words, with their muskets cradled in the crook of their arm Pahotan and the young warrior began walking towards the encircling forest. Needing little encouragement, pulling sharply on the halter rope of the lead horse, with the remainder of the brigade the collective name for a party of fur-traders strung out behind him in single file Blessing followed after them.

Watching from their hiding place, the two young Seneca warriors waited until the last horse had disappeared from view then turning their backs on the lake they melted away into the dark-green bosom of the forest.

All morning the brigade moved deeper into the primeval forest the scaly trunks of the giant trees towering over them, dark and foreboding. The cloying smell of decaying pine needles clogging their nostrils. Occasionally a shaft of golden sunlight would pierce the dense canopy and lift their spirits, while the enduring silence prayed on their senses. Thankfully as they neared the Genessee River the forest became noticeably fresher. With the evergreen firs and mature hemlocks giving way to elms and oaks, the woods took on new colors as daylight filtered through their spreading branches. Midday found them splashing across a wide stream, its banks thick with bayberries and ground-vine. After stopping in mid-stream to allow the horses to dip their muzzles into its cooling waters, with the redolent smell of wood smoke pervading the air they pressed on to the far bank and the hillside beyond. Heartened by this glimpse of civilization they were even more delighted when reaching the crest of the hill, pointing towards a distant slope planted with rows of squash and maize Pahotan called out "Tiataroga." This was his village. They had reached their destination.

Less than an hour later as they approached the outlying longhouses of the Seneca village, as if by magic a crowd of noisy, naked children, some carrying a naked baby on their hip, came scampering towards them. Their coal-black eyes wide with excitement. Following on their heels, snarling and barking were a pack of lean camp dogs with their fur on their necks bristling with anger. Although none of these mischiefs had ever seen a horse before they were not at all overawed by the sight of such large animals. Some, mostly boys showing how brave they were by running up and touching them. The bolder ones among them even ducking under the horse's bellies before scampering away, shrieking with delight at their daring. But it was the horse's legs that interested the dogs. That was until Doublejohn convinced them otherwise by swinging his foot and catching two of them with the toe of his boot. Sending them scampering away with their tails between their legs. Not known for his conviviality, Blessing surprised his companions by scooping up some of the younger children in his arms and setting them down on each of the horses. Laughing out loud as they began shrieking with a mixture of terror and delight. Clutched the animal's mane with their hands, and clinging on for dear life, their skinny legs wrapped around the animal's neck.

"See how they love's it, John-John? See how they love's it?"

With little doubt that he was referring to the horses as well as the children, Doublejohn let the intended rebuke die on his lips with a half-smile.

With Pahotan striding out ahead of them, reaching the outlying long-houses the fur-traders and their entourage were immediately surrounded by a swarm of women dressed in their all-alike doeskin dress. Chattering excitedly in high-pitched voices while craning their necks for a good view of the traders. Each of them was eager to know what trinkets, and baubles were in their packs. Keeping to the fringes of the crowd, haughty and aloof their menfolk, mostly warriors looked on with measured indifference. They had been told of the traders's imminent arrival by the two young warriors when they returned to the village two hours earlier. Thanks to them they also knew each of these Yengeese traders as though they had seen them with their own eyes.

At twice the size of the other long-houses, the council house's gloomy interior was illuminated by tallow candles, their feeble light reflecting off its elm bark walls. Each section of the building secured by lines of upright wooden stakes, its arched roof, blackened by smoke from countless fires supported down its spline by rows of stout wooden posts set at regular intervals. At its center was a large smoke hole, the light from it pooling in a yellowish circle on the rush mat flooring. Seated on a low bench in front of a shallow fire-pit, the flickering flames illuminating their faces were several tribal elders. Old men, their keen deep-set eyes gleaming in their sockets. Their stern features betraying little emotion. Each wore a gaudy blanket draped over his naked shoulders, with necklaces, and amulets fashioned from the claws of wild animals and the bones of small birds hanging around their necks. Standing before them on the other side of the fire, was Kiashuta, a chief from a neighboring tribe. His bold features daubed in ochre and soot. His head was clean-shaven except for a mane of hair reaching down to his broad shoulders. Hanging from a chain around his neck was a silver gorget. A trophy looted from the body of a dead English officer. Gathering about him were three other warriors, their faces streaked with war paint, a tomahawk or a war club hanging from their belt. When he spoke his voice was strong, his words emotive. His speech concluded, turning to one of his cohorts Kiashuta reached out and took the cloth bundle he was holding in his arms. Carefully unfolding it he revealed its contents; a belt crafted from purple and black shells, and a blood-stained tomahawk. With the tokens of war displayed for all to see, snatching up the tomahawk, with a wild yell Kiashuta flung it down at the feet of the Elders.

Slowly Wapontak, the tribal chief climbed to his feet, a shaft of sunlight striking him like a beam from a spotlight. He was a tall man with bold, crafty features. The scars on his broad, hairless chest were a testimony to his bravery in battle. His thigh-length leggings embellished with the scalps of his enemies. Hanging from the belt around his waist were a scalping knife and hatchet. Expressionless he stood for a moment looking down at the bloody axe. Then in one fluid movement pulling the blanket off his shoulders with a dramatic flourishing, he threw it over the offending object. With the blood-stained axe hidden by his blanket, Wapontak gazed across at the warriors standing before him. His expression carved in stone.

"Do you think us fools that we would believe your lies?" He said in a rising voice, his words laced with venom. "These French you speak of are far away and growing smaller, and the English have their foot upon their neck. Can they give my people blankets, kettles, gunpowder, and shot? No, only the English can give us these things, and yet you would have us take up the hatchet against them. I say go away from us now before the anger in my heart swallows you up."

Seething with rage, throwing down the war-belt Kiashuta whirled about, and followed by two of his warriors he began striding towards the doorway. The third warrior, his face disfigured by a patch of scar tissue where flames had burned away the flesh, snatching up the rejected tokens before hurrying after them. Pausing in the doorway, he stared back at Wapontak, his scarred face twisted into a malevolent mask, then pulling aside the curtain he was gone. Witnessing the departure of Kiashuta and his emissaries, eager to impart their news, their lithe bodies still glistening with sweat the two young Seneca warriors made their way towards the group of elders. Looking on from the shadows, disappointed by the proceedings, Shingas listened to their words with mounting interest. News of the fur trader's imminent arrival filling his invidious mind with hope. A hope that where Kiashuta had failed they might be the ones to furnish him with a chance to restore his reputation as a war chief.

Outside, enveloped by the entourage of excited Seneca with Pahotan leading, the fur traders and their packhorses made their way through the village towards the quadrangle at its centre. Enclosed on three sides by orderly rows of long-houses, except for what appeared at first glance to be tree trunks the large square of barren ground was completely uninhabited. There were three of them, grouped in a triangle with ten yards or so separating one from the other, their height ordained by an axe some eight feet above their roots. It was only on closer inspection that the reason they were there became clear. They were burning posts. Instruments of torture, their charred trunks a testimony to the horrors inflicted on the poor souls unfortunate enough to have their fate decided in such a manner. Carrying a long wooden bench between them two warriors emerged from the council house. Setting it down in front of a large rush mat which had been laid out on the ground they disappeared back inside. Moments later squinting in the bright sunlight Wapontak, emerged from the building, and accompanied by the elders, in formal procession they made their way to the bench. Seating himself at its center, with the elders jostling for position alongside him Wappotak beckoned to a group of warriors. With the last of the elders seated, and the party of armed warriors positioned behind them like a guard of honor all was ready. Old men they may be, but these tribal elders were venerated above the fiercest war chief and held in high esteem by every member of the tribe. Their social status was assured. Their past exploits were an inspiration to every young warrior.

With Pahotan at its head, the unruly procession crowded onto the quadrangle. All noise subsiding as they flowed around its edges, a quietness settling over the throng of spectators. Even babies were hushed. Nothing, not even the yapping of a dog intruding on the silence. Beyond the trilogy of blackened stakes, Soule watched as Pahotan crossed to where Wapontak was seated. Straining to hear what was said as the warrior whispered into the sachem's ear. Then, with his message delivered, striding across to the council house Pahotan slipped inside. Emerging moments holding a pipe, its long stem adorned with the wing feathers from a Jay. Returning to Wapontak he placed the lighted pipe into the elder's outstretched hands. Well versed in tribal etiquette, taking this as his cue, walking forward Soule seated himself cross-legged on the rush mat. Behind him his men began helping the children down from the horses, watching as they scampered away into the waiting arms of their mothers. Placing the mouthpiece of the calumet peace pipe with its carved stone bowl between his lips Wapontak inhaled a mouthful of the aromatic tobacco. Exhaling, he passed the pipe to the man seated on his left. The elder following his example before handing it to the man seated next to him. The pipe passed from one elder to the next until the ceremonial ritual was completed. With the pipe returned to him reaching out his arms Wapontak offered it to Soule. Taking the proffered pipe, putting it to his lips Soule dragged in a mouthful of smoke. Letting it out again like a sigh before returning the pipe to the Sachem. With the welcoming ceremony completed turning towards the watching traders, Soule gestured with his hand.

Aware of his role in the proceedings, making his way to one of the horses, Baily removed a small bundle wrapped in a blue cloth from one of the packs. Walking across to Soule, winking knowingly, he handed it to him. Placing the bundle on the ground in front of him, Soule untied the binding. Unfolding the blue cloth corner by corner, revealing its contents to the inquisitive gaze of the elders. Leaning forward, Wapotak ran his eyes over the array of gifts; a pair of bone-handled knives, twists of tobacco, leather pouches filled with powdered paint, a different colour in each one, and a string of purple shells. Emotionless, he climbed to his feet, and raising the calumet aloft in a strong voice he began addressing the traders. Speaking in the dialect of his people, knowing that at least one among these Yengeese would understand his words.

"You have come at last Englishmen. In the forest of the Onondowaga, you are strangers, but we welcome you for you are the good men among your people, not ones who anger me."

Slowly Soule climbed to his feet. Standing for a moment he looked around at the sea of faces surrounding him. A feeling that once again they were putting their head into the lion's mouth pervading his thoughts. But when he spoke, he did so with confidence. Well aware that timidity would be seen as a sign of weakness by such a capricious audience.

"We are glad of your welcome." He called out. "We are indeed strangers, but we have left our footprints in the forest so that we may find our way again. We have walked far. From the shores of Lake Oneida, pointing with an arm towards the north. Our legs are weary, but our hearts are glad."

Murmurs of approval rippled through the crowd. Ever the showman Soule paused for a moment. He was beginning to enjoy himself. But when he spoke again, he did so in a more serious tone of voice.

"I know there have been Frenchmen here." An assumption at best as the only evidence he had was seeing the two warriors who had acted as their guides using French shot to wager with at the previous evening's gambling. "But I am pleased that you have closed your ears to their lies and have welcomed us as brothers." Pausing to allow the murmuring to subside. "These French are jealous of our great friendship. They would lie and spread false tales, then cheat you off your furs. We bring you good trade. We still hold tightly to the chain of friendship that the Iroquois and the English have long held. Not once has it fallen from our hands."

With his eyes fixed on Soule Wapontak listened intently to his words. He was surprised that these Yengeese knew that Frenchmen had been in his village. But he was not concerned by it. Angered only by the man's hollow words when speaking of the chain of friendship which existed between them. In truth, the English walked with a broad and heavy foot upon the lands of the Iroquois. The officers and soldiers of the forts within the boundary of their lands treated their chiefs and warriors with contempt and abuse. There were already those among the Seneca who talked of war against the English before it was too late. Before like the French they too were "kicked out of the way". He also remembered that it was these same bad Frenchmen who had brought guns and blankets to his village in the winter. They had been a help to his people when the English with-held their customary presents to his people. Caring little for their suffering even though they knew they had come to rely on them for their very existence. It was true that these same "Coureurs de bois" also came seeking to incite his warriors against the English. Warning how they would neglect them, steal their lands and finally destroy them unless they and all the tribes of the Iroquois nation rose up against them. Urging them to use the guns they had brought against them before all was lost. Although aware that these seeds which had been planted with malice were now beginning to grow into truth, seeing the laden packhorses Wapontak was reminded of the needs of his people. So, swallowing his bitterness, his face devoid of expression he replied in a firm voice.

"Our ears hear your promises. Your words are welcome but among us, promises must be seen with the eye, and only then can they be believed." His carefully chosen words a mild rebuff to the traders lies.

Heeding the murmurs of unease which greeted the Sachem's words, seeking to reassure the watching crowd Soule moved across to the line of packhorses. Calling out in a raised voice as he began patting their packs in time with his words.

"See we bring you powder and shot. Warm blankets, and fine, sharp knives. Hatchets, red cloth, tobacco. Whiskey to wet your throats. Hawks-bells and beads for your women."

No sooner had Soule fallen silent when one of the elders, his thin body wrapped in a red blanket, climbed to his feet.

"You bring us no guns." He called out in a reedy voice, pointing at Soule with a bony finger. "These Yengeese bring us no guns."

Although startled by the old man's words Soule was prepared for the accusation.

"Flute bring me your cups and fetch down one of the barrels." He called out before turning to face his accuser. "Yes, it is true we have no guns to trade. But hear me. We do not know your villages. We do not know who lights the welcoming fire or who would light fires to burn us in. Are we such fools to bring guns to those who could be our enemies? To hold them out saying kill us? No, first we must see the faces of our true brothers, only then can we give them guns to fight their enemies."

Even before Soule finished speaking, Flute had already removed the bung from one of the barrels and was splashing the raw whiskey into the three tin cups. Pushing one of them into the outstretched hands of Wapontak, and the remaining pair into the grasping hands of two other elders.

Putting the cup to his lips the old Sachem swallowed down a mouthful of whiskey, the fiery liquid burning his throat. Taking a second swig before passing the half-empty cup to a waiting elder. Watching enviously as the man gulped down a mouthful of the spirit. Finally, one of the cups reached the one who had spoken out, and gulping what remained of the liquor in a single swallow, he gestured for more. Snatching the battered tin cup from him, Flute began filling it to the brim with whiskey. Better to let the old fool get drunk than have him cause any more trouble.

Finally, satisfied that they had enough free whiskey, replacing the bung Flute hammered it home with his fist. Seeing that there was to be no more whiskey on offer, with the tin cup still gripped in his hand, Wapontak climbed a little unsteadily to his feet.

"My people", he called out, the effects of the whiskey slurring his words. "These Yengeese have come among us with much to trade. Go now and bring out your pelts and furs. Show them what great hunters you are. Also, let fires be lit so that they may fill their bellies, and know that the Haudenosaunee The Six Nations are still their brothers and that the ancient chain of friendship is still held tightly in our hands."

Immediately a great shout went up from the assembled crowd and with his words dying away, whooping and yelling the crowd began dispersing. The people running off in all directions like children let out from school.

Just as quickly but in a more orderly fashion, Soule and his men began stripping the horses of their heavy packs, spreading the trade goods out onto blankets in orderly rows. With every man benefiting from a share of the profits, great care was taken with their presentation. Whether a string of beads or a hatchet, every item was displayed to good effect. A display designed to tempt the most reticent buyer into parting with his furs. A little way off, anticipating early customers Flute and Linnet had already removed the lids off two of the barrels. Standing cup in hand ready to measure out a helping of "firewater" in exchange for a beaver pelt or some other exquisite fur.

With the horses freed of their packs, surrounded by a troop of mischievous children, Doublejohn led the weary animals away from the encircling long houses. Finding a suitable spot at the edge of the forest, securing a tethering rope between the trunks of two trees, he began hitching each of the horses to it by its halter reign. This done, sack in hand he began shaking out what was left of the oats onto the ground in front of each animal. Satisfied that the horses were settled, and in no danger of being pestered by inquisitive children Doublejohn made his way back to the quadrangle. He regretted that there had not been more provender for his charges, but doubtless, a trinket or two would be enough to secure a suitable supply of corn for their next feed.

Gripped with excitement, her pretty face radiant with bear oil and vermilion, Minawa began weaving her way through the throng of people. Heavily pregnant she moved slowly, her doeskin dress, decorated with colored beads stretched tightly across her distended abdomen. Having never seen a paleface man before, or set eyes on a horse the thrill of encountering both in a single day was intoxicating. After pausing to catch her breath, drawing back the curtain she stepped into the dimly lit long-house. Running down the center was an aisle some six feet wide, with rows of small equally spaced compartments down each side. Each separated from its neighbor by a partition fashioned from boards made from bark, held in place by wooden stakes driven upright into the ground. Ducking into one of the rooms Minawa reached for the bundle of furs lying on the floor. Threading her fingers through the strip of rope that held them together. But the moment she attempted to lift the heavy bundle a sharp pain knifed through her stomach. Freeing her fingers, she pressed both hands across her navel. Clamping her teeth together to suppress the cry threatening to burst from her mouth. Then, like an apparition Shingas appeared at her side. Angered by her stupidity he glared down at her. Startled, she looked up at him, instantly regretting her foolishness. Admonished, she lowered her gaze, watching as Shingas picked up the heavy bundle of furs, and without saying a word he began striding towards the doorway.

When Shingas and Minawa eventually reached the quadrangle, it was already a hotchpotch of activity. People coming and going, their strident voices adding to the general hubbub. Cooking fires tended by wizened old grandmothers with limbs like sticks dotted the open ground. At two of them, a large kettle filled with corn porridge warmed its bottom in the flames. At others, cuts of meat burned or went uncooked depending on which side was facing towards the flames. Those charged with attending to its cooking it too busy, chattering to worry over such a nicety. Weaving their way through it all were dozens of half-naked children, their noisy outbursts accompanied by howls from the pack of camp dogs adding to the clamorous din. Before long scores of other poker-faced warriors, their cache of pelts carried in their arms or loose bundles over their shoulders began arriving. Congregating around the traders, with discerning eyes they began examining the trade goods spread out on the ground to tempt them. Close on the heels of these successful hunters were their wives. Round-faced maidens got up in all their finery. Their jet-black hair shiny with bear grease, their high cheeks powdered with vermilion. Each of them hopeful of some new adornment. Mingling among them, her eyes bright with anticipation Minawa viewed the assortment of trinkets and baubles laid out on the blankets. Each display as alluring to her as the trays of diamonds, and rubies on show in a jeweler's shop window would be to a high-born lady.

Away from the melee, a large crowd of warriors gathered around the whiskey barrels. Each clamoring for a cupful of whiskey. All eager to exchange an exquisite fur for a swallow of the fiery liquid. Off to one side, a group of older women looked on with trepidation. Knowing from experience the bouts of madness the evil water would soon inflict on their menfolk. Some of the more cautious ones returned to their rooms and hid their knife and tomahawk out of sight. Emboldened by curiosity, the two young boys began weaving their way through the legs of the warriors gathered around the whiskey barrels. Approaching the one manned by Linnet, holding out their hands, palms cupped they began begging him for a drop of the liquid. Amused by their impudence, just as Linnet was about to give them a taste, Flute suddenly grabbed him by the arm. Cursing the lad for his intended stupidity, while at the same time swinging his foot at the two scallywags and sending them scampering away.

Hunger was also a magnet, and with the aroma of hominy, and roasting meat permeating the breeze-less air, people began gathering around the fires eager to satisfy their appetites. Confident enough to leave the others to manage the business of trade, Soule had already been lured to one of the bonfires and was soon helping himself to a meal. Smiling, as he sliced a cut of meat from one of the carcasses roasting over the fire, at the two naked children sitting inches from the dancing flames, chewing contentedly on the titbit their mother had given them.

But it wasn't only the children who attracted Soule's attention. His gaze was also drawn towards the four warriors standing in a tight group beside one of the long houses, each armed with a musket, their savage faces emblazoned with war paint. Detached from the activity around them, hidden at times by the clamor and confusion of the moment, when he was permitted a good look at them, he found himself filled with a sense of unease. Then suddenly they were lost from his sight. Blotted from view by the myriad, of sparks sent flying up into the air when one of the women dropped a bundle of sticks onto the dying fire. When the air eventually cleared, they were gone. Vanishing from sight as quickly as a dream. Disappointed, turning away from the fire Soule made his way towards the large crowd gathered around the trade goods, his thoughts occupied by the four warriors. Something about their presence concerned him, and he was not a man to be easily worried.

Perched high up on the outstretched branch of a withered oak a pair of ravens, the bright sunlight reflecting off their glossy wings looked down with beady black eyes on the scene of activity below them. It was a roost they often frequented, so they were not at all alarmed by the noise and commotion. At least it meant they would not be troubled by young boys shooting at them with hard-tipped arrows. It seemed today these young archers were too busy with other things to bother about using them as target practice. Although prompted by curiosity, the real reason for their visit was watching the women going about the camp catching and killing young dogs for the fire. In the past four days, their only meal had been what little they had managed to scavenge from the carcass of a deer picked clean by wolves. With the plaintive whines of the luckless ones carrying up to them, they surveyed the scene below them. Watching the old woman as she drank the warm blood spilling into her cupped hands from a dog's throat. Observing her as she went to work with her skinning knife before impaling the carcass on a spit suspended over the fire. Seeing the groups of young girls returned from the woods their basket filled with berries and wild fruit. Watching the young boy with the puppy clutched in his arms dashing away into the forest. Nothing escaped them. But what mattered most, what captured their attention were the discarded entrails, entwined like a writhing mass of mating vipers lying beside one of the fires. A prize so tantalizingly close yet so dangerous to claim. Waiting patiently, when the chance came with the bravery of eagles they swooped down. Cawing in triumph as they snatched up a beak-full of glistening entrails. Their powerful wingbeats lifting them high into the air.

Marked out by the livid patch of burned flesh which scarred his face, the warrior pushed his way through the jostling throng surrounding the whiskey barrels. The naked blade of his knife pressed against his side. Flute and Linnet were doing good business, the pile of pelts at their feet evidence of their success. While all around them, clutching a gourd or other such vessel in one hand, and a pelt in the other more Seneca warriors clamored to be served. Forcing their way through the melee of early drinkers who having downed several cups were quickly succumbing to the sensations of drunkenness. At the center of it all, his sleeves rolled up Linnet dipped his tin cup into the barrel of raw whiskey. Absorbed in his task he turned to serve his next customer. Smiling in amusement at the sight of the two warriors staggering towards him on unsteady legs, their angry voices rising above the din. Following a step behind them, taking advantage of the distraction, brushing aside the two inebriated warriors, the scar-faced warrior plunged the blade of his knife deep into the lanky youth's chest. Stunned by the force of the blow, his face clouded by a look of disbelief Linnet staggered back, blood gushing from the deep wound in his chest. He tried to scream but no sound came, and then his legs buckled under him, pitching backwards against the barrel. Slumping onto the ground a sound emerged from his open mouth. Not the scream he had hoped for, just a low moan. Then his body began convulsing, jerking and twisting as though wracked by an epileptic seizure. Moments later, the spasm passed, and with his thin lips drawn back in a macabre grin, the whiskey from the overturned barrel pooling around him Linnet passed from life to death. With a last look at the murdered trader the scar-faced warrior melted away into the encircling crowd, the knife clutched in his hand, its blade dripping with Linnet's blood.

Alerted by Flute's scream, pushing aside anyone barring his way Soule raced across the quadrangle. Even before he reached the barrels, seeing Flute standing alone, the crowd pulled back as though the trader was surrounded by a ring of fire, Soule feared the worst. Then as he drew nearer, he saw the overturned barrel with Linnet"s body stretched out beside it. The lad's hands clutched to his chest. His lifeblood running in rills along his bare arms and forming a puddle on the dry ground. Dropping to his knees beside him Soule ran his fingers across Linnet's eyes. Although death was nothing new to him it still left its mark. Like a notch cut into a pole. With some, many of whom he had killed himself he had felt no emotion. To him, they were just another stick for the devil's fire. But with Linnet it was different. Here there was real sadness. There was also a feeling of guilt. An admission that he should have given more credence to his sense of foreboding. The knowledge that he should have done better by him pricking his conscience. Like a trapped animal, Flute confronted the encircling ring of Indians, then dropping onto one knee he pressed his lips to Soule's ear, his breath stinking of whiskey.

"There was a shouting row, I didn't see it start but when I looked, I seen this painted heathen with his knife pushed into poor Linnet's chest. T'was nothing I could do Quinty", he said, choosing to call the man by his first name. "I knowed he was done for."

Soule simply nodded his head. Although he hadn't witnessed the murder, he already knew more about its perpetrators than Flute. He couldn't admit to it of course, and even if he did what use would it be? None. Just as there was no point in asking Flute to point out the culprit. To identify the one who had carried out the murderous act. He would have already made his escape, the bloody knife clutched in his hand like a trophy. No, for now, his duty was to ensure that the same fate didn't befall them all.

"Stay with him." He said to Flute, quickly climbing to his feet.

It was then that he saw Bailey, Doublejohn and McCallum, each clutching their muskets pushing their way through the crowd. Crowding around him, grim-faced the three men stared at the multitude of people milling around them. Each of them expecting to hear the shriek of the war cry at any moment.

"Steady lads", said Soule, sensing that matters could quickly get out of hand.

No sooner had he spoken when he saw the figure of Wapontak, flanked by a dozen armed warriors striding purposefully towards him. The crowd parting to let them through. Walking alongside the old Sachem, his war club resting lightly in the hollow of his arm was Pahotan. Approaching the group of traders Wapontak fixed his gaze on the over-turned whiskey barrel with the body Linnet sprawled on the ground beside. Seizing his chance, Soule stepped forward.

"Do you see what has happened here?" Soule shouted, pointing an accusing finger at Linnet's corpse. "One of my men is killed.

Murdered by one of your warriors." His voice ringing with anger. "Are we all to be killed is this your bloody plan?"

Calmly, the old Sachem listened to the man's vehement outburst, his emotions concealed behind an impenetrable mask. He knew this was the work of Kiashuta. That his black heart had conjured up this deed in the hope of in-flaming his warriors into an orgy of killing. Before responding to Soule's accusation, he turned towards Pahotan, speaking urgently in a low voice. Nodding in acknowledgement Pahotan gestured to the group of warriors and turning away he began jogging towards the narrow path leading into the forest. Alone and unguarded Wapontak turned to face the angry trader, his right hand placed over his heart, a gesture designed to assure the listener that the words he was about to speak were truthful.

"No one among my people has committed this evil thing. This is the work of those who would have us take up the hatchet against our brothers the English." Pausing he stretched out his arm, pointing towards the forest. "I have sent my warriors to find the ones who did this and to bring them back to answer for their crime."

Convinced of the old Sachem's lack of complicity in what had happened, Soule slowly nodded his head. What the elder had said was true. The four savages he had observed were obviously the troublemakers the old chief had spoken of. The ones he had failed to keep a better eye on, and who, thanks to his negligence now had a bloody trophy to display because of it. But before he could reply a sudden disturbance in the crowd distracted him, and turning his head, he saw Blessing emerging from the throng of people. Fearing the man's reaction when he caught sight of Linnet's body, Soule began striding towards him. Hoping to reach him before he saw the lad's prostrate body. But he was already too late.

At first, Blessing just stood and stared. His simple mind failing to comprehend what he was witnessing. And then he saw the youth's blood-soaked chest, and all became clear. With rage welling up inside him like bile, consumed by the desire for revenge and with a primeval roar Blessing lumbered towards the old sachem. His hand instinctively reaching for the hatchet stuck in his belt. Taken by surprise at the speed of Blessing's reaction, Soule rushed towards him, blocking his path.

"Hold back you fool", said Soule, driving his shoulder hard into the man's bear-like chest. "Would you have us all killed?" Gripping Blessing's wrist as he spoke.

But his plea fell on deaf ears, and with anger fueling his strength, struggling to free his axe Blessing began pushing Soule aside. It was then that he felt the sharp pain in his side, just below his ribs, and he knew instantly he had been stabbed.

"I'll kill you fore I let you pass", said Soule. "You know I mean it."

It wasn't so much the venom in Soule's voice that stopped him in his tracks. It was knowing that he would do it too, which brought Blessing to his senses. That, together with the wound in his side was more than enough to deflate his anger. Freeing his wrist from Soule's grip with a resigned look, Blessing turned away, and with ponderous steps, he made his way towards Linnet's body. The lad had been his good and dear friend. In truth, although few knew of it, he had been more than that, and although forced to swallow his desire for revenge Blessing knew that if he were patient, an opportunity for retribution would present itself. That if he bided his time Linnet's death would not go unavenged, he would see to that. So, with his watery eyes fixed on the youth's pock-marked face, the mask of pain replaced by a look of calm repose, with effortless ease he lifted him off the ground, and cradling Linnet's body in his powerful arms, turning away from the upturned barrel Blessing slowly walked towards the encircling forest. His bearing as dignified as any undertaker.

With Linnet's murder no longer a distraction, dismissed like a storm in a teacup, together with their women groups of warriors began drifting back to the cooking fires. The late-comers crowding around the dwindling piles of trade goods, haggling over some cherished item. Freed from restraint, with their mother's busy chattering among themselves children returned to their boisterous games. Set apart from the comings and goings, confronted by a group of warriors, each clamoring for a cup of the fiery liquid, blotting the memory of Linnet's death from his mind Flute removed the lid from a third barrel. Returning to the business at hand, the blood-soaked ground the only evidence of the young trader's fate. Standing aside, with mixed emotions Soule watched as Blessing disappeared into the gloomy woods. Although filled with sadness at the lad's untimely death, he was also angry with himself. Angry at his failure to prevent it. To a man, they were each aware of the dangers imposed on them by the very nature of their employment. An acceptance that death was sometimes the price they had to pay for their chosen occupation. But Soule took little comfort from it. Not long after, as though to compound his regret he watched as Pahotan and his warriors emerged from the forest. The fact that they were alone told him all he needed to know. That the ones responsible for Linnet's murder had escaped, and the chance to punish the guilty party was lost.

Watching the women as they moved through the village in search of dogs for the fire, with the puppy clutched in his arms, crossing the wide ditch which surrounded the village the young boy disappeared into the forest. Threading his way through the trees within minutes he reached his favorite hiding place at the foot of an ancient hemlock. The tree had died long ago but in the act of falling it had become snagged in the outstretched branches of its neighbors. Its rotting branches formed a trellis-work for vines and creepers to exploit. Sunlight peered in through the torn canopy, its yellowing fingers exploring the length of its decaying trunk. Exposed by its half-drawn roots, ferns and wildflowers had taken root prospering in the rich, black mould. On hands and knees, his puppy held tightly against his chest the boy burrowed under the trespassing foliage until he reached a bower formed by the tracery of entwined stems and stalks. A gloomy arbor, dark and damp but a fine hiding place for a small boy and his puppy.

Sitting cross-legged on the ground the boy strained his ears, but beyond their secret place, the world was silent. The only sound came from the puppy's tongue as it licked his face. Sensing that the young dog was hungry, removing a morsel of meat from the pouch suspended around his neck; an old tobacco pouch which had belonged to his grandfather, he dropped it into the puppy's mouth. The last thing he wanted was for it to begin whining. And so there they stayed, hidden and silent for what was for ones so young, a very long time. Eventually though, with the puppy's struggles growing stronger, the boy crawled reluctantly out from the hiding place. Fearing that there might still be people whose hunger needed satisfying, rather than risk returning to the village, with the wriggling puppy held tightly in his arms he walked away into the surrounding forest. He had almost reached the small clearing where he knew they could play in safety when the boy was suddenly stopped in his tracks by the sight of a figure straddling the trail ahead of him like a colossus. The body of a man held in his arms. Alarmed by the man's sudden appearance, the boy's first instinct was to run away. But then he recognized him. He remembered seeing him that very morning lifting the young children onto the backs of the strange animals. And so, reassured by the memory and curious as to why he was carrying another of the Yengeese in his arms, he stood his ground. Taken by surprise at the child's sudden appearance, thankful that he had not run off, lowering Linnet's body onto the ground with a wave of his hand Blessing beckoned to him.

"Come up lad. Come close and see a dead man. Toddy here won't mind you staring."

Although he didn't understand what the man had said the gesture was plain enough, and with curiosity overcoming caution, the struggling puppy gripped tightly in his arms, the young boy walked towards him. Of course, he had seen a dead body before but not one like this. Not the body of a Yengeese. It was then as he stood staring down at Linnet's bloody chest that the puppy's struggles intensified, and wriggling free from the boy's arms it scampered off into the trees. Instinctively, the boy turned to give chase but even before he could move his legs Blessing's powerful hands closed around his neck like a choking collar. Terrified, his eyes bulging with fear the boy lashed out, frantically trying to free himself from the man's grip. But his fate was already sealed. The beating of his small fists against Blessing's chest as futile as a butterfly's wings on a pane of glass, and with a twist of his wrists Blessing snapped the boy's neck like a dry twig. Lowering the child's lifeless body onto the ground without a flicker of remorse, lifting Linnet's body in his arms Blessing continued on his way.

He had barely gone a dozen yards when the thought struck him, and turning around, his gaze fixed on the body of the dead child he pondered its merits. Thankfully it wasn't a difficult conclusion to reach, even for Blessing, and with his mind made up he retraced his steps. Yes, he would bury them here. It was a good enough spot, and it suited his purpose well enough. Pleased with his decision, pushing aside the overhanging branches Blessing dragged the two bodies into the gloomy interior of the trees. Finding a suitable spot, he began digging into the rich soil with his axe, clawing away at the soft mould with his fingers. It was hard and sweaty work, and although the wound in his side had begun bleeding again, he worked on tirelessly. Eventually, satisfied with his efforts resting his back against the heaped earth Blessing dragged mouthfuls of air into his lungs. But his rest was short-lived, there was still the burial to attend to. Linnet was the first to be put into the grave, his lanky body fitting snuggly in the measured hole. Then the child, his frail body stretched out face uppermost on Linnet's bloody chest. Taking a moment to survey his work, with uncharacteristic tenderness, leaning down Blessing kissed Linnet on the lips. A lover's farewell. With the simple ceremony concluded Blessing began filling in the hole. Heaping the earth into the familiar mound, firming it with his hands before scratching Linnet's name into the soil with the blade of his axe. His work done, pushing aside the dense foliage Blessing immerged onto the narrow trail. Accustoming himself to the sudden brightness, he stood for a moment and looked around for the boy's puppy. Why he wasn't sure, after all the animal would make a poor witness. Amused by the thought, pushing the axe into his belt with lumbering strides he made his way back to the Seneca village.

Already the day was ageing. The clamor of trading had ended, and calmness had settled over the village. Weary children rubbed their tired eyes. Indolent warriors lounged about the dying fires, while those who had drunk their fill at the whiskey barrels lay where they had fallen, sleeping off the effects of their indulgence. Seated in doorways their hands and tongues rarely still, mothers and grandmothers took their ease. Only the snarling of scavenging camp-dogs intruded upon the air of tranquility.

Outside the entrance to the long-house which was to be their lodgings for the night McCallum, Flute and Doublejohn busied themselves by sorting through the bounty of bartered pelts. Not a single bead or blanket remained of the trade goods. Even the whiskey barrels were empty, drained of their fiery contents. Putting away his tally-paper Soule watched as the skins and pelts were sorted into manageable bundles. Although pleased with the good business they had done he was also conscious of the mood of melancholy, which hung over his men following Linnet's death. Sensing in the urgency with which they worked, how eager each of them were to be gone from this place. Then he heard the sound of Baily's voice. And while what he was saying was unclear there was no mistaking the anger in its tone. Horrified at the prospect of another death, Soule hurried towards its source. Rounding the side of the long-house to his horror he saw Baily, confronting a Seneca warrior, the trader's hand resting on the handle of his axe. Hurrying over to them, knotting his hands in Baily's coat front he dragged him aside.

"Are you gone mad?" Said Soule vehemently, staring hard into the man's face. Unable to find a reply, Baily simply lowered his head. Allowing his anger to subside, releasing his hold on the man's jacket Soule turned to face Bailey's antagonist. Swaying yet never quite losing his balance, his savage features stripped of their menace Shingas fixed his bleary eyes on the man now standing in front of him. The pelt of a winter fox gripped in his outstretched hand.

"Whisky! Whisky!"

Although the words were slurred, Soule understood the warrior's request.

"There is no whiskey. Whiskey is gone." Soule replied in a firm voice.

Perplexed, Shingas shook his head slowly from side to side, and holding out his arm he pointed to the three whiskey barrels.

"Whisky!"

Without bothering to reply, pulling his axe from his belt Soule walked across to the barrels. Tipping one of them onto its side, with a single powerful blow he, staved it in.

"Whiskey is gone! No whiskey!" He shouted, hoping that the demonstration had convinced the warrior that the barrels were empty. Then snatching the proffered fur from the warrior's grasp Soule thrust the axe into his hand. Bleary-eyed, Shingas focused his gaze on the hatchet. It felt good in his hand. Thankful that his trade had proved acceptable Soule returned to where his men were busy securing the last of the bundles into bales.

"Come lads it's time to fill our bellies."

Eager to comply with his suggestion, the traders filed into the long-house. As was customary a meal had already been prepared for them. A show of hospitality, the tantalizing aroma of freshly roasted meat permeating the air. Seating themselves beside the fire each man quickly set too with his knife. Slicing off lumps of meat and stuffing it into their mouth. The flesh of dogs basted in oil and cooked over an open fire was as appealing to them as an oven-roasted quail marinated in red wine, and garnished with sprigs of Rosemary and Thyme would have been to an English aristocrat.

With the axe clutched in his hand, Shingas staggered away. The feeling of pleasure at his trade was quickly lost, consumed by the mood of depression which possessed him like an evil spirit. Like other members of his race, the Seneca found little happiness in their drinking. Maudlin sorrow or violent rage were the only rewards for their indulgence. With the strength in his legs ebbing away, and only his will power stopping him from falling to the ground Shingas staggered towards his long-house. The tinkling bell of consequence warning him that he must find his couch before this sickness consumed more of his faculties. It was then that he saw Minawa standing with a group of young women, her newly acquired blanket draped over her shoulders. Strutting about them, done up in plumes and beads were half-a-dozen youthful dandies, their lithe bodies anointed with scented oil. Each of them basking in the flirtatious glances of the young maidens. Eagerly, Shingas' invidious mind went to work, distorting the naturalness of the scene, refuting its harmless nature. Jealously welling up in him at the thought of the young men paying his woman compliments with their eyes. Aroused, he became its plaything, and screaming out in anger, his legs found new life Shingas ran towards them. Startled by his sudden appearance the young men stared at Shingas in disbelief. Moments later he was among them, striking out blindly with his axe. Terrified, the young maidens began fleeing in all directions like chickens being chased by a fox. The youthful gallants, without the ties of warriorhood to bind them quickly followed suit. All except for one. With his pride overcoming his fear he stood his ground. A focus for Shingas' rage.

Horrified, Minawa watched as Shingas lunged at the youth, his axe carving murderous arcs in the air. With a wild cry, she rushed towards him. Reaching out she gripped her husband's upraised arm, pleading with him to stop. Incensed, Shingas lashed out at her with his free arm, the blow sending her reeling backwards onto the ground. Agile as a cat, in an instant Minawa was back on her feet. Arms outstretched, she ran towards him, her voice, her whole being imploring him to stop. Blinded by rage, and deaf to her desperate cries, raising his axe in the air Shingas lashed out at her. The steel blade sinking into her head. The force of the blow dropping her down onto her knees. Freed of his youthful pride by this murderous act, turning on his heels the young dandy began running towards the safety of the encircling long-houses. Freeing his axe, seemingly oblivious to Minawa's lifeless body lying on the ground like a child's discarded doll, blood gushing from the terrible wound in her head, Shingas chased after him. But after only a few strides his false strength began ebbing away, and after a short stumbling run his legs finally gave way. Pitching him forward against the corner of a long-house, his head striking the corner post.

Later, with the village cloaked in darkness, gathering up Shingas' inert body in their arms Pahotan, and another warrior carried him back to his long-house. Laying the unconscious figure on his couch, dismissing the warrior Pahotan seated himself on the vacant cot. He had barely settled himself when an old woman appeared in the doorway, her lined face etched with concern. Sending her on her way with a wave of his hand Pahotan pulled a blanket around his shoulders, and with the bloodied axe resting in his lap, he began his vigil.

The moment he opened his eyes Shingas was greeted by a painful throbbing in his head. Raising his hand, he touched a finger to the swelling above his left eye. The epicenter of the pain which lanced through his head with the regularity of a heartbeat. Racked by thirst he reached for the earthenware pitcher beside his couch, pressing it to his lips he drank greedily. Gulping down mouthfuls of the water. Grateful for its coolness on his raw, dry throat. Having quenched his thirst, as he placed the pitcher onto the ground, he suddenly noticed the figure seated on the cot opposite him. Recognizing who it was, before Shingas had a chance to speak Pahotan reached out his arm and handed him the blood-stained hatchet. Taking it from him, Shingas stared down at the bloodied axe, his mind struggling to fathom its relevance. Then slowly, his memory revealed its significance. Images of the part it played during his moment of insanity flashed before his eyes like a macabre slideshow, instantly enveloping him in feelings of sadness and remorse. The knowledge of what he had done burning like a fire in his brain. But even in the shadowy darkness of his room, such emotions were not allowed to manifest themselves. Only anger was allowed to reveal itself. Blighting his face before running like quicksilver into his coal-black eyes. Only anger could free him from the feelings of guilt which threatened to envelope him. True born, not some apparition of the whiskey barrel. In his invidious mind, he was blameless. It was these English dogs who were the guilty ones. They had poisoned him with their whiskey, and because of it, he had lost everything. So, in the blinking of an eye anger transmuted into an overpowering desire for revenge. Climbing unsteadily to his feet, slipping his carry-all across his shoulder Shingas picked up his musket and powder-horn, and with a final look at the bloody axe, he walked out through the open doorway.

Seeking the sanctuary, and solitude of the woods as he was making his way through the silent village Shingas was stopped in his tracks by the sound of women's voices. The tuneless words of their mournful eulogy permeating the early morning air. Drawn towards the long-house the sound was emanating from, even as he reached for the curtain covering the doorway, knowing what lay behind it he knew he couldn't pull it aside. To peer into the building's candle-lit interior and see Minawa laid out on a low Cot her body dressed in her finest clothes, all traces of blood washed from her face. Her hair combed to hide the terrible wound in her head would be too much for him to bear. Besides this, nothing must be allowed to increase his sadness or remind him of his guilt. His only thoughts must be of finding a way to take revenge on those he held responsible. A terrible vengeance for Minawa had been with child, and now both were gone.

With familiarity guiding his steps, following a narrow path, Shingas made his way through the forest. Ethereal specks of sunlight dancing among the towering hemlocks like mischievous fairies. The cathedral hush broken by the distant yelping of a vixen calling to her mate. Midday found him at the edge of a gloomy cedar swamp, the quaggy ground littered with the prostrate trunks of decaying trees. Scattered among them like confetti were clumps of sweet-gale their bright orange catkins sparkling like jewels in the occasional splash of sunshine. Skirting its edges Shingas followed the narrow trail as it climbed away before him along a steep wooded ridge. Reaching a point where the path levelled out, his path was blocked by a recumbent bolder. A huge granite rock partially overgrown with ferns, and lichens with rivulets of water trickling across its weathered surface from the hillside above. Removing a beaded tobacco pouch from his carry-all, approaching the boulder Shingas carefully placed it on the stone's crystalline surface. Pausing for a moment, he retraced his steps to where a rocky outcrop afforded him some concealment, and seating himself cross-legged on the hard ground he fixed his eyes on the giant rock. Other gifts had also been placed on its craggy surface. Pushed into crevices or laid on a narrow ledge, a child's moccasins. An earthen-wear pot filled with wild honey. A string of freshwater pearls. Each item placed there as an offering to a deity. A gift to a supernatural spirit in exchange for an answered prayer.

All that day and into the early evening sitting stiff-backed, his musket across his knees Shingas gazed upon the pagan alter. The gift of tobacco he had left was for Areskoui, the God of war. It was his help that he invoked with fasting and prayers. But sadly, no dream had come. No vision was revealed to him. It seemed Areskoui's face was turned away from him. Eventually, fearing that the fur-traders might have already left the village, he abandoned his vigil, and with his hopes dashed, consumed with malignity and frustration Shingas set off through the darkening forest. His life was pictured with gloom. His standing and reputation as a war-chief were lost. Not a single warrior would snatch up the tomahawk after hearing his cry for vengeance. But like others of his race, Shingas was possessed with an inordinate pride, a pride which denied these adversities. As a warrior of the Haudenosaunee The Six Nations, he would have his revenge. Nothing would stand in his way. This desire for vengeance was now his life's ruling passion, and he would brave anything even death itself to satisfy its craving. So preoccupied was he with these vengeful thoughts, that it seemed the small sound had escaped his ears. But there it was again, the plaintive whimpering of a young dog.

Even in the partial darkness beneath the spruce branches, Shingas' eyes found the puppy. It had unearthed one of the boy's small hands, the forbidding marker guided him to the grave. Dropping onto his knees Shingas began clawing away at the mounded earth with his hands, and in minutes its terrible secret was revealed. Reaching down he gently lifted the boy from the shallow pit and cradling him in his arms with uncharacteristic tenderness he brushed away the dirt which still clung to his innocent face. Gazing down at the small lifeless figure he knew that here in the stillness of the child's heart was Areskoui's answer to his prayer. This foul murder would not go unpunished. No ears would be closed to the cry for retribution, and he, Shingas would use the moment to avenge the loss of his wife and child. Thrilled by the thought, grabbing the puppy by the scruff of its neck he pushed aside the overhanging branches, and with lengthening strides, Shingas made his way along the narrow trail leading to the village.

Bathed in the moonlight, with the young boy's lifeless body cradled in his arms Pahotan slowly walked between the rows of longhouses. An hour earlier, Shingas had slipped unseen into the village, and seeking out his old ally he had told him what he had found. Horrified by Shingas' revelation accompanied by two trusted warriors Pahotan returned with him to the macabre grave. All that day there had been great concern over the missing child. Bands of warriors had searched the forest while beating on their drums and chanting mystical incantations the elders had called upon the Great Spirit for his help. Many feared that the child had been carried off by an evil spirit in the guise of a wild beast. While others voiced the possibility that a Huron or Ottawa war-party in search of scalps, had kidnapped the boy. No one could have suspected this terrible thing. As Pahotan made his way through the silent village, as if by magic warriors and their women began appearing, the lurid glow from their flaming torches illuminating the darkness. Their discordant cries, accompanied by the howling of the camp-dogs rending the air. Suddenly, a toothless old crone with sunken cheeks began forcing her way through the throng towards him, closely followed by a young woman, her face lined with anguish. With a soulful cry, the woman wrenched the child from Pahotan's arms crushing his frail body to her chest. Sobbing with relief, she called out his name but there was no response. And then realization swept over her. Her child was dead. With an agonizing scream, she sank to her knees, her tears wetting his marble face. In moments gentle hands led her away. Other hearts seeking to share her grief.

Then sounds began again. People called out in angry voices. "Where had the child been found? How had he died? Tell us! " Tell us! They shouted. Raising his arms in the air, Pahotan called out to them, and immediately an expectant hush descended over the crowd. Beyond the ring of people waiting like actors in the wings of a stage the two warriors, each holding onto one of Linnet's legs, awaited their cue. Choosing his moment, with a wild yell Pahotan called out to them, bringing them into the tragedy. Stone-faced, dragging Linnet's rigored body behind them like some gruesome plough the two warriors emerged from the darkness. Incited beyond restraint by Pahotan's revelation of what had happened to the child, with bloodcurdling shouts the crowd swarmed around Linnet's corpse. Hacking at it with knives, sticks and tomahawks. Amid the frenzied attack, groups of women began arriving carrying armfuls of wood, quickly heaping it into a pyre. After setting it alight, shrieking like demons, the virulent mob tossed the trader's mutilated corpse into the flames, leaping around the fire in an ecstasy of loathing. Standing in the shadows, the firelight playing on his face drinking in the orgy of hatred Shingas witnessed his hopes for vengeance becoming a reality. Satisfied with his work, unnoticed, Pahotan slipped away, and crossing the quadrangle he made his way to the council house. Pausing at the entrance for a moment, he pulled the heavy curtain back and stepped inside.

Seated on the low bench in the center of the building Wapontak stared into the embers of the dying fire. Seated beside him, their blankets wrapped around them against the chill night air were a handful of tribal elders. Emerging from a corner of the gloomy building an old woman began feeding sticks into the fire, the dying flames licking hungrily at the wood, their flickering glow ebbing outwards in a pool of mellow light. Touching a burning tapper to the bowl of his pipe Wapontak sucked a mouthful of tobacco smoke into his lungs, watching as the plumes of smoke drifted upwards into the dark void beneath the arched roof. Satisfied that the pipe was lit, gesturing with his hand he beckoned for Pahotan to come forward. Seating himself on the rush mat across from the old sachem Pahotan began his address. Running his eyes over the old men as they listened attentively to his words. When he spoke, it was without magniloquence; it was enough that he lied to them. Only telling them what he wanted them to hear. He and two others had found the boy's body buried with the murdered trader. Yes, it had been hidden with great cunning, but Tusonderongue had found it. Even the moose trembles when he is in the woods. No mention could be made of Shingas' part in all this, to bring him into it would only jeopardize their motive for revenge. Any suggestion that he wanted to use the boy's death to satisfy his own act of revenge would quickly be seized upon by the old sachem and used to forbid any retribution being taken against the English traders. With his small black eyes stabbing at Pahotan through the swirling pipe smoke Wapontak listened attentively to his web of lies, anger welling up inside him. He was angered by the senseless killing of the child. Angry that he was powerless to contain its violent consequences. Although only one of the traders was a murderer, each of them was condemned for his actions. So instead, he concerned himself with precautions, and when he spoke this thought was paramount. None must know of what had become of these Yengeese traders. Nobody must know of his people's part in their deaths.

"Hear me." said Wapontak, his words delivered with great solemnity. "We cannot know who is the guilty one so all the whiskey-carriers must be killed, and their bodies carefully hidden. It must be as though they had been a dream."

"If they fight, they are too few. If they run away, we will catch them", said Pahotan, mindful of the old sachem's concerns. "All will die, and when the rain comes, and washes away the marks of their horses even the dream will be forgotten." His sagacious reply touching a chord in each of the elders and reminding them of when they too were warriors.

Nodding his head in acknowledgement, with a heavy heart Wapontak watched as Pahotan climbed to his feet, and with purposeful strides, he made his way to the darkened doorway.

Having been informed of the elder's decision camp-criers began moving through the village. Their raised voices called those warriors who belonged to the same clan as the mother of the dead child to the war-fire. She belonged to the totemic clan of the wolf, and by virtue of the Haudenosaunee custom of decent following the female line so too did her child. Inside Pahotan's long-house, half-hidden in the shadows Shingas watched the comings and goings of the women as they busied themselves carrying out the preparations entrusted to them, feeding the starveling fire with wood. Placing trenchers filled with meat, and any other food that could be gleaned after the gluttony of yesterday onto rush-mats.

Finally, with their work done, they filed outside. Pausing in the doorway one of the young maidens turned towards Shingas a coquettish smile on her face. He was a warrior without a wife now and she hoped his eyes had looked upon her with pleasure. Admiring her boldness Shingas stared back at her, his eyes lingering on the shapely contours of her body. Then in an instant she was gone, her heart filled with hope.

No sooner had the women departed when the warriors of the wolf clan began arriving, each adorned in their savage finery, their scalp-locks fluttering with feathers. Their bold features, and lithe bodies smeared with paint. Red for war. Black for death. A tomahawk and scalping knife pushed into their belts. By feasting on the food which had been prepared for them, each giving his solemn promise to avenge the murder of the child. With his savage features freshly painted for war, licking the grease from his fingers Shingas looked at the warriors gathered around him. Unwittingly their revenge would also be his, for in his simple mind the fact that he belonged to the same clan as the murdered child was not purely a coincidence but a true manifestation of Areskoui's will.

With their feasting over, heads held high the war-party walked in stately procession to the quadrangle. Awaiting them, crowded around its edges was a savage audience Pressing forward expectantly, fearful of missing the smallest sight. Moments such as these rescued their lives from boredom, and although it was late into the night all thoughts of sleep were pushed aside. Only babies were allowed to close their eyes. At the center of the clearing a large bonfire was already burning, its flames bathing the on-lookers' faces in warmth and light. Driven into the ground beside it was a tall post, its rough surface daubed in red paint. Suddenly a great cry went up, and with Pahotan at its head, the war party filed into the circle. Walking beside him, basking in the moment, Shingas was suddenly distracted by a movement in the crowd as a young woman, her hair adorned with a brightly colored ribbon pushed her way to the front. Smiling flirtatiously as he passed in front of her. Intrigued, Shingas stared back at her, his stoic features masking his interest. Unsettled by his lingering gaze, averting her eyes Meeataho turned away, melting back into the crowd, her heart fluttering like a trapped bird.

Armed with a knife and hatchet, in a loud voice Pahotan began haranguing the attentive crowd. Recounting with savage eloquence his prowess as a warrior. Enacting his exploits in a primitive pantomime. Striking the post as if it were an enemy and tearing the scalp from the head of the imaginary victim. Incited by his performance, one after another the warriors of the war-party followed his example. Boasting their renown, they rushed up to the post, striking it with their tomahawks, and startling the night with the shriek of the war-cry. Leaping and dancing in untamed spontaneity they circled the fire, its brightness creating grotesque giants of their shadows, its flames inspiring them. Inebriated by the emotive scene, the watching crowd suddenly surged forward into the circle, their fearful cacophony resounding into the sepulchral darkness of the forest.

CHAPTER FIVE

It was an hour before dawn when Soule woke, he had slept badly so he was glad to be awake. Stretched out around him, barely discernible in the false light the remainder of the brigade lay like logs in their blankets. Without a word, he moved among them rousing each of them with his foot. The first to stir was Doublejohn. Conscious of his duties, picking up his sack of fodder he made his way to where the horses were tethered and began feeding each of them a handful of corn. With no appetite for lighting a fire, breakfast was the cold remains of last night's supper; some dry strips of meat, and a few moldy oat cakes washed down with water from the nearby stream. But nobody complained, to a man they had caught Soule's mood of foreboding and were also eager to be on their way. Willing hands quickly loaded the heavy bales of furs onto the horse's backs, and with the last strap tightened they moved off in single file into the trees.

All morning, they trudged through the vast forest. Through its stillness, its towers of bark the narrow trail running ahead of them like a will-o-the-wisp. The going was hard, and Soule set a cruel pace, but it was only Doublejohn who complained, and then only from concern for his beloved horses. But with his protests falling on deaf ears, he eventually gave up and the brigade pressed on in silence. It was the horses who heard the stream first, long before the men caught sight of it at the bottom of the steep hillside. The silver flashes of sunlight on water glimpsed through the crowded trees. To everyone's relief, Soule called a halt beside its rushing waters, a chance for a brief rest before pressing on towards the Genessee River which he hoped to cross before nightfall. With Doublejohn and McCallum attending to the horses, mindful that they didn't drink too much, the others plunged their heads into the stream, gulping in mouthfuls of the pure cool water. Refreshed, dipping a grubby hand into his kitchen sack, Flute removed the last of the moldy journey cakes, and a few dry-tack biscuits, offering them to any that would take them. Not one to be put off by a little mold, Bailey quickly scooped up a handful of the cakes, stuffing them into a pocket for later. Others who were tempted by the biscuits taking the precaution of soaking them in the stream first rather than run the risk of losing a tooth. All hoping as they chewed on their meagre meal, that once across the river their captain would let them kill a deer. Wiping the crumbs from his mouth with his coat sleeve gesturing for Baily to step aside, Soule whispered something into the man's ear. Confidant that the man had understood his instructions, eager to be under way he turned to the others.

"Time to move out lads."

In single file with each man holding onto a lead rope the brigade and its laden packhorses forded the fast-flowing stream. Re-joining the narrow trail as it hugged the side of the gently sloping hillside before disappearing into the unbroken forest beyond. When the last of the packhorses had disappeared from view, wading into the purling waters, hidden by the archway of foliage Baily began splashing his way upstream. Reaching a spot where the water deepened as it swept around the base of a rocky outcrop, slinging his musket over his shoulder, using imperfections in the rock as handholds he began clambering up the rock-face. As he neared the top, he found his progress impeded by the overhanging branches of a tree. With no way around it, as he pushed them aside, one of the branches became snagged in his coat pocket, a tear appearing in the coarse material as he tugged it free, sending the broken pieces of cake cascading onto the rocks below. Cursing the loss of his meal, brushing aside the offending branches Baily dragged himself up onto the summit of the craggy rock. Pausing for a moment to catch his breath, unslinging his musket he moved away into the serried ranks of trees. Finding a spot which offered him a good view of the fording place, with his back against the trunk of a tree, pushing a hand into his torn pocket, Baily removed the paltry remnants of Flute's cakes and began stuffing them into his mouth.

At dawn, with Pahotan leading the war-party emerged from the long-house and walking in single file they made their way through the deserted village, and into the surrounding forest.

Waiting to greet them as they entered a secluded glade were several women holding a musket and a powder-horn. Each of them stepping forward and handing them to their respective warriors; a husband or a son. While receiving in return any prized amulet they wished to leave in their safekeeping. Standing among them, unsure how her audacity would be received, summoning up her courage Meeataho stepped forward. Recognizing the maiden from the previous evening Shingas stared into her face, his features softening as he took his accoutrements from her. Overcome with joy that her boldness had been rewarded, with her heart pounding, turning gracefully on her heels Meeataho ran across to re-join the other women. Her claim to his affection revealed for all to see. With each warrior now armed for war, after firing their muskets into the air, the discharge Pahotan, and the war-party moved away into the forest.

Effortlessly the war-party jogged through the dark labyrinth of trees. The hoof prints left by the packhorses made the trader's trail easy to follow. Although it was obvious from the length of the animal's strides that the brigade had hurried, it was still early morning when they came upon the remains of the trader's night camp. Dropping onto one knee a warrior pushed his hand into the grey ashes of the dead fire, their warmth telling him all he needed to know. Confident that the Yengeese would soon be under their knives, like a pack of hounds with the scent of their quarry in its nostrils, the war-party moved off. Passing the piles of fresh dung left by the horses before disappearing into the crowded trees.

An hour later they reached the place where the traders had forded the stream, and with an opportunity to quench their thirst several warriors began making their way towards the bank, only to find their path blocked by Shingas. These Yengeese were no fools, and Shingas knew that if they wanted their scalps, it was wise not to underestimate their cunning. And so, with the war-party looking on he made his way to the fording place and began examining the confusion of tracks left by the traders, and their pack-horses. Minutes later, confident with what he had learned, wading across to the opposite bank Shingas began running his eyes over the trail of footprints leading away from the water's edge. Satisfied with his discovery, re-crossing the stream he revealed to Pahotan what he had learned. Six of the Yengeese had entered the stream but only five had reached the other side. Beckoning to Tusonderongue and Cattawa, the same two warriors who had dragged Linnet's corpse into the village, Pahotan made them aware of Shingas' suspicions. Eager to discover if the Yengeese traders had indeed left one of their numbers behind, handing their muskets to another warrior the pair made their way towards the stream.

With its eddying current, littered by boulders making it to treacherous to follow downstream, shrouded by the overarching trees side by side the two warriors waded upstream. Their keen eyes scouring the steep rocky banks on either side for anything incongruous. Any sign that would betray where the trader might have left the stream in search of a hiding place. It was Tusonderongue who found the evidence; the tell-tale fragments of cake scattered over the mossy boulders at the base of the rock like confetti. Gesturing to Cattawa, with the agility of a mountain lion, the pair began climbing the outcrop, each determined to be the first to reach its summit. Happy to share the honors, pulling their scalping-knives from their belts they began following Bailey's telltale footprints into the forest. Moving like shadows through the labyrinth of trees they quickly found their intended victim lying full-length on the ground, his attention focused on the path leading away from the fording place. In an instant Tusonderongue was on him, straddling Bailey's prone body like a bareback rider. His free hand forcing the man's head down into the damp mould. Unable to cry out a warning, instinctively, Bailey reached out for his musket. But even as his hand closed around the barrel Cattawa's foot stamped down on its wooden stock, pinning the rifle to the ground. With his fingers knotted in the trader's greasy hair Tusonderongue plunged his knife into Baily's neck, its honed blade slicing through flesh and tendon. The fur-trader's body convulsing violently as his muscles contracted, his lifeblood spurted out from his ruptured throat. Holding him down until the spasm had passed, freeing his blade from the deep wound Tusonderongue pushed its tip into the skin above Bailey's ear. Slicing through the flesh in a circular motion around the crown of man's head before peeling away the fur-traders scalp. Wiping the blade of the bloodied knife on Bailey's hunting-frock Tusonderongue climbed to his feet, his gruesome trophy gripped in his hand. Then with their murderous work done, plundering the dead man's body, leaving Bailey's corpse to the mercy of scavenging animals, the two warriors made their way back towards the stream.

Unaware of Bailey's fate, with their buckskin shirts stained with sweat, the brigade pressed on through the dark recesses of the forest, hugging the bank of the fast-flowing stream as it meandered ahead of them through the trees. Cursing their luck when without warning, its racing waters suddenly plunged into a deep ravine, its steep rocky sides cutting like a scar into the wooded hillside. Left with no option, bowing to its capricious nature, with the roar of the raging stream in their ears following the narrow trail, the brigade struggled up the steep incline. Below them, glimpsed through the foliage of ash, and maple their curving trunks anchored to the rocky walls of the precipice by their roots, the raging waters raced onwards to a meeting with the Cohocton River.

Having circled around the hillside, concealed among the trees the war-party watched in silence as strung out in line the fur-traders made their way along the trail below them. Choosing his moment, Pahotan cried out, the war-parties muskets exploded in a ragged volley. The wasting hail of musket balls striking traders and horses with impunity. First to die were Flute and McCallum, both men staggering under the impact of the musket balls before falling to the ground mortally wounded. Up ahead, unharmed by the deluge of deadly missiles, Doublejohn watched in horror as one of the packhorses, blood spurting from the bullet wounds in its neck began side-stepping towards the ravine. Instinctively, he grabbed hold of its lead-rope desperate to halt its progress. Whinnying in terror the fear-crazed animal edged ever closer to the precipice. Despairingly, Doublejohn pulled on the rope. But the animal's strength was too much for him, and unwilling to release his grip he was dragged over the edge. Man, and horse plummeting to their deaths in the raging cataract below. Uninjured, Soule watched as the remaining panic-stricken horses began moving ever closer to the edge of the narrow trail, and the yawning chasm below. Knowing that his life depended on it, knife in hand Soule raced towards them, and grabbing the lead rope of the nearest animal he sliced through the horse's girth strap. Dragging the heavy packs of the animals back, hauling himself onto the horse, with a despairing look towards the prostrate bodies of his men, kicking hard with his heels he urged the terrified animal into a run.

On the hillside above, throwing aside their muskets, the war-party raced down the slope towards the stricken traders. The chilling sound of their war-cries reverberating off the steeply slopping sides of the ravine. With blood oozing from the bullet wound in his shoulder, Blessing turned to face the oncoming warriors. Planting his feet he raised his musket and singling out the leading warrior he fired. Watching with satisfaction as the musket-ball struck the warrior in the center of his chest, dropping him to his knees like a pole-axed steer. But all too quickly another warrior was on him, his tomahawk raised above his head. Instinctively, Blessing lashed out with the butt of his musket, sending the luckless warrior staggering backwards, his hands clutched to his bloodied face. Undeterred, the remaining warriors closed on him. Having singled him out as the likely child killer they meant to take him alive. Well aware of the horrors that awaited him should he fall into their clutches for Blessing the choice was a simple one and turning his back on his enemy he strode across to the edge of the ravine. Musket in hand, arms outstretched, with a defiant yell, he threw himself headlong into the abyss. His bear-like body falling like a sack of grain onto the rocks below. The stream's foaming waters plucking his lifeless body from their weathered surface and carrying it away downstream. His arms and legs snapped like twigs as it ran the gauntlet of jagged rocks.

From his vantage point among the trees, Shingas watched his vengeance manifesting itself as the warriors of the war-party charged down the sloping hillside towards the dead and dying traders. Then from the corner of his eye, he spotted the horse moving along the trail below him, a man clinging desperately to its back. Throwing up his musket he aimed and fired. Watching with satisfaction as the horse's front legs suddenly buckled under it, pitching its luckless rider headlong onto the ground. Eager to have his moment of revenge as he pulled his knife from his belt Shingas suddenly hesitated. Standing a dozen paces away, tomahawk in hand he saw Cattawa watching him with envious eyes. Mindful of the part the young warrior had played in his plan, meeting Cattawa's gaze, Shingas gave a consenting nod. With a wild cry, Cattawa raced away down the slope towards the stricken fur-trader. Dazed by the fall, shaking his head from side-to-side Soule slowly pushed himself up onto all fours. But before he had a chance to climb to his feet Cattawa was on him. Striking downwards with his tomahawk, its steel head sliced into Soule's upturned face with sickening force. The gush of blood transforming it into a crimson mask. Drinking in the moment Shingas watched as the young warrior pulled out his knife and went to work on Soule's scalp. Holding the trader's matted scalp aloft and shrieking out his war-cry.

With the bodies of the remaining traders thrown into the ravine, Pahotan gathered the war-party around him. Having avenged the murder of the child, with the body of the dead warrior strapped to the back of the one surviving packhorse he was eager to return to their village. Standing apart from proceedings, Shingas and the four young warriors grouped around him looked on, their minds on other things.

"Come! It is done", Pahotan called out to him. "We go back."

"For you, it is done but for me, it is not finished." Shingas replied. "I do not go back." A hint of anger in his eyes. His words uncompromising. Knowing that trying to convince him otherwise would be useless, Pahotan turned his gaze to the two warriors standing at Shingas' side. Although he had once had their loyalty, he knew that they too would not be swayed by his words. The fresh scalp hanging from each of their belts had whetted their appetite for more, and he knew they would go with Shingas. With nothing more to be said, Pahotan walked across to the edge of the ravine.

Below him, the bodies of the five fur-traders littered the jagged rocks. The stream's eddying pools stained with their blood. Soon wolves would find them, and feast on their flesh. Then scavenging foxes and wolverines would carry off their bones. Even the wild trout would play their part. Rising from the deep pools among the rocks and feeding on any morsels washed down to them on the swirling current. Soon nothing would remain of them, and their horses, and with only the trees to bear witness to their deaths, they would soon become a dream. And in time even the dream would be forgotten.

CHAPTER SIX

Samuel Endicote had chosen the spot well. Situated in the lee of a broad valley and fed by a wide stream meandering through a meadow of grass as tall as a man's waist. Surrounded by an abundance of forest fit for tar and lumber it would make a fine homestead. There were some among the more, timid souls who had chosen to remain in Norton who said he had been foolish. Headstrong even, in venturing across the Oswego River, and into the wilderness beyond with all its dangers. But Samuel had paid them no heed. It had been the desire for a new life not temerity which had caused him to uproot his family from the relative comfort of a home in the Shires, and sail across a wide expanse of ocean in a ship whose leaky timber meant hours at the pumps just to keep her afloat. It was with an eye to the future not a whim that had brought him to this fertile valley. That, and a desire to be his own man. To forge a better life for himself and his family away from the restraints and shackles of the old world. Also, a man with four sons had a duty to repay God for such a blessing. To have a thought for their lot, and should the chance arise the courage to set the bearers of his lineage on a sound and righteous course.

Standing at the heart of the farm was a single-story cabin constructed of logs caulked with mud; each laid out horizontally, interlocking at the corners. Topped by a shingle roof, inside its three rooms were of a good size. The largest having two small windows with a single window in each of the others. Its only entrance was through a solid door made from thick oak planks set on iron hinges. A stone chimney held together with mortar dominated the end wall, giving the building a look of permanence. Alongside the cabin enclosed by a tall picket fence was a kitchen garden, its dark, fertile soil planted with pumpkins, carrots and turnips. Across from the main house was a large barn constructed from planks of sawn timber with a pair of stout doors set in its center. A storeroom for the harvest yet to come, and home to a dozen hens. Facing the south side of the barn was the beginning of a smaller cabin. Its log walls and roof timbers set in place but as yet without shingles, windows or a door. Behind it, half as deep as a man's body was a sawpit with piles of tree trunks, all stripped of their branches, stacked up beside it. Surrounding it all, enclosed by a split-rail fence was an acre of cultivated ground planted with Indian corn with a further acre of pasture for the pair of Devon oxen and a milk cow.

The first year had been hard. The bitter cold of winter had turned the ground to iron, and while spring had thawed it in time for planting, the fickle English corn had refused to ripen. Worse yet their three hogs had died of the fever. But with the warmth of summer came new hope, and the crop of Indian corn they had planted now grew up straight and tall, its golden ears promising a bountiful harvest to come. The forest too had yielded up a wealth of good timber which now lay trimmed and sawn into planks of uniform length. All neatly stacked inside the barn awaiting transportation to Norton where it was sure to fetch a good price. And so seated in his high-backed chair by the evening fire smoking his pipe Samuel Endicote looked back on his bold endeavor with pride. He had secured a future for his sons" and this rich fertile valley would be their inheritance.

Adam's welfare had long been a concern to him but now with the prospect of his impending marriage to the woman Esther, even this burden was lifted from his shoulders. The thought that it might well be a childless union had troubled him a little but with three more sons to sire him grandchildren he felt confident that his lineage was assured. Besides, although she was no beauty, he had seen the desire in Saul's eyes when he gazed at Mistress Colwill. He had also heard him on more than one occasion tiptoeing to her bed in the dead of night. So, he knew with some certainty that it would not be too long before she bore Saul's bastard. Morally of course the thought abhorred him, but his conscience was appeased by knowing that at least the child would have Endicote blood in its veins. The only mystery was that it hadn't already happened.

Emerging from the surrounding forest Kit paused for a moment, squinting his eyes against the sudden glare of sunlight. At the age of ten, he was the youngest of the Endicote's four sons. A tall gangly lad with a sunburned face and long straw-colored hair. His over-size shirt, one of his elder brother's cast-offs tucked into a pair of homespun breeches. With his eyes accustomed to the sudden brightness, slinging his squirrel-gun over his skinny shoulder, with Pharaoh, a large black and tan hunting dog bounding ahead of him he began running helter-skelter towards the farm. Clearing the split-rail fence in a single leap with his tongue lolling out from his mouth Pharaoh waited patiently as Kit clambered up and over the stout lengths of wood. Reunited, flanked on either side by the ordered rows of corn, the pair then made their way towards the cabin. A thin wisp of smoke rising from its chimney like a cat's tail.

Spotting the boy and his hound emerging from the cornfield through the half-open barn door, freeing herself from Saul's embrace Esther began buttoning up her bodice. Puzzled by her actions Saul looked at her quizzically.

"What's wrong?"

"Kit is coming."

"You worry too much", said Saul, reaching out for her. "He'll not come in here."

"He may do", said Esther, pushing his hands away. "We must be careful."

Sensing her insistence, scowling angrily Saul moved away into the shadowy interior. With the last button in place, picking up the basket of eggs lying at her feet, after taking a moment to compose herself Esther pushed open the heavy barn door and stepped outside. Casually falling in beside Kit as he walked on passed.

"Your Ma has been calling for you", said Esther.

Kit looked sideways at her. Hoping to see that she was teasing him.

"You've been off in them woods again, haven't you?"

Kit dropped his head. Although she was right, he was determined not to admit it.

"You know your Pa forbids it." Said Esther, a hint of sternness in her voice.

"You won't tell, will you Esther?" pleaded Kit, knowing he'd been found out. "Please say you won't tell."

Turning her head Esther looked down at his wretched face.

"I might. It all depends." Said Esther, her resolve weakening.

Reaching the cabin, knowing that Esther wouldn't really tell on him just as Kit was about to reward her with a smile the door was suddenly flung open, and there framed in the doorway was the imposing figure of Mrs. Endicote. She was a large powerfully built woman with bright piercing eyes and a chest like a pouting pigeon. Her greying hair pulled back behind her head and held in place by a knotted ribbon giving her a matronly appearance. Judging by the frown on her face she was clearly not in a very good mood.

"I declare girl I've never known anyone take so long to fetch a few eggs", she said, spitting out the words without fear of being answered back.

"And you, you young scallywag", she went on, turning her attention to Kit. "You're never here when I need's you. Be off now and fetch your brothers to the table."

Thankful for being spared a tongue lashing or worse for his absence, turning on his heels Kit began running towards the saw-pit, his faithful hound bounding along beside him. Watching the boy as he raced away, with a huff of displeasure, her hands tugging at the front of her apron, Mrs. Endicote flounced back inside. A relieved Esther following a step behind her.

Barely a mile away from the isolated farm, walking in single file Shingas and his small war-party moved through the gloomy forest. Threading their way through its dense pine thickets and clambering over the decaying carcasses of prostrate tree trunks. Eventually, with the ground sloping away before them they entered a stand of golden beech trees, the late afternoon sunlight permeating their extending canopy. It was there that Tusonderongue made his discovery. Dropping onto one knee he began examining the patch of earth. His finger carefully tracing the tell-tale outline of a child's footprint impressed in the soft mold. Moments later Cattawa raised his arm. He had found the paw prints of a dog.

With the meal over, while Mrs. Endicote busied herself at the stove Esther began clearing away the cups and plates. Putting any scraps of meat into a wooden bowl for Kit's dog. Although there was work to be done Saul and his brother Joshua, a head shorter than his older sibling but endowed with the same good looks, remained seated. After such a hearty meal they were in no hurry to return to the sawpit, and the seemingly endless supply of logs awaiting their attention. Sadly, their moment of relaxation was cut short when an inner door opened, and Samuel Endicote, accompanied by his eldest son Adam, walked into the room. Resembling his father in height and build, Adam had his mother's countenance, all except for the eyes, for while hers were like two bright buttons, his were pale, and listless giving his face a doleful look. Like all the men of the household, he wore a loose cotton shirt, buckskin leggings and a pair of sturdy leather boots. With the clock on the mantelshelf striking the hour Samuel turned to his wife.

"We'd best be leaving."

With a faint smile, Mrs. Endicote nodded her head in agreement.

"What's this then", said Samuel turning to the two idlers lounging at the table, a note of anger in his voice. "Finished our days labor, have we?"

Sheepishly, the two young men looked up at him but said nothing.

"Bring up the wagon. Look lively now."

Obediently, Saul and Joshua got to their feet, and without a word, they left the room. With the door closing behind them, clutching a leather satchel, Mrs. Endicote crossed to her husband, and slipping the strap over his shoulder she pecked his cheek with her dry lips.

"I've packed a slice of venison pie for you both, and a little of the cake left over from supper. Doubtless Minister Rathbone will provide you with supper, so twill suffice till then." Her tone of voice emphasized the fact that there would be no more provisions even if he chose to ask.

Over by the window, Esther busied herself with the washing-up. Rinsing each item in a bowl of hot water before stacking it on the crude wooden draining-board. From the corner of her eye, she caught sight of Adam hovering by the door watching her. Hoping she would look up and see his smile. Seeing he was to be disappointed he turned away and followed his father outside.

Standing in the shadow of the overhanging branches Shingas and his war-party looked down on the farm nestled in the valley below, their sharp eyes missing nothing. Satisfied, handing his musket to Cattawa, Shingas moved out from among the trees, and made his way towards the meadow of wild grass at the foot of the sloping hillside. Reaching the stream, he followed its winding course until it reached the edge of the cornfield. Splashing across its pebbled bed, guided by the split-rail fence with the stealth of a predatory animal, he moved towards the cluster of timber buildings.

Harnessed to the hitch-pole of the wagon, their heads pestered by a cloud of flies the two oxen waited patiently as whip in hand, Samuel climbed up into the seat alongside Adam. Taking up the thick leather reigns, nodding a farewell to his wife Samuel turned towards his three sons standing in a group awaiting their patriarch's impending departure.

"No idleness while I'm gone, do you hear? " His voice as always imbued with authority. "Yon cabin needs finishing before the week is out. See to it I'm not disappointed."

Shuffling their feet Kit, and Joshua remained silent. Leaving it to their elder brother to speak up on their behalf. Taking advantage of their reticence, looking across towards the cabin Saul gazed across at Esther standing in the doorway. Although her forthcoming marriage to Adam suited him well enough, for reasons he couldn't altogether understand just recently he had begun to find the arrangement wholly disagreeable to him. Perhaps if he had not been such a stranger to the feeling, he might have recognized that the cause of this conflict of emotions was simply jealousy.

"Aye father", said Saul, returning his thoughts to the matter in hand, "we'll see to it that the newly-weds have a roof over their heads before their wedding night." A hint of undisguised amusement in his voice.

Ignoring his son's sarcastic reply, eager to be on his way with an encouraging crack of the whip, and shouts of "Hey up! Hey up!" Samuel set the wagon in motion. The team of oxen strained against the yoke as they lumbered forward. The wagon's four iron-rimmed wheels following the deeply rutted track leading away from the farm. A track which would eventually take them across the river to the small settlement of Norton.

Without waiting until the wagon was out of sight, turning away the three brothers ambled towards the sawpit. Lagging behind his brother's Kit cast a forlorn look over his shoulder at Pharaoh, chained to his post outside the cabin. Recalling his disappointment at his mother's words as she fastened the chain to the hound's brass studded collar. "There'll be no wandering off into yonder woods for you and your hound while your fathers away. Do you hear? "

Pleased with his reconnaissance, with mounting interest Shingas watched the wagon as it rumbled away from the farm. Eager to follow its progress, slipping back into the meadow he made his way alongside the split-rail fence. The waist-high grass rippled in his wake as he moved away towards the encircling forest. Once among the rigid spires of spruce and fir dropping down from the high ground, jogging at a steady pace through the thinning trees Shingas followed the rutted track eastwards towards the distant settlement of Norton.

It was another hour before the laden wagon reached the river. A nameless tributary of the Oswego, its broad eddying current flowing silently beneath the arching foliage of maple and ash. Sensing the animal's reluctance, raising his whip Samuel drove the reluctant team into the ford, the swirling waters quickly reaching up to their bellies. Urged on by his shouts, and the crack of the whip, their tongues lolling from open jaws, the panting oxen hauled the cart up the far bank, and into the dark bosom of the forest beyond.

Hidden in the deep shadows beneath the towering trees, motionless as a statue Shingas watched as the cart disappeared from his sight. With darkness falling, confident that the wagon would not be returning until morning, turning his back on the river he began following the rutted track back towards the Endicote's farm.

Located on a wide expanse of cleared ground beside the Oswego River at a point where it narrowed between low banks, the shallow water and stony bed making it an ideal place to ford, the small township of Norton prided itself on being the most westerly of the settlements. Its single street lined on both sides by cabins, and the occasional two-story clapperboard house a testament to its growing importance. The light from their window lamps, and porch lights illuminating its hard-packed surface. Situated at the far end was the town's forge, its furnace glowing with a bright orange light even at this late hour. The clang of the blacksmith's hammer ringing out like a church bell as with sweat, and craft he worked his magic on the length of heated iron resting on the horn-tipped anvil.

With a final crack of the whip, Samuel urged the oxen up the sloping bank and into the street, eventually bringing the wagon to a halt in front of a wide windowless building fronted by a pair of heavy doors. Set above them, just visible in the closing darkness was a length of whitewashed board with the words "Zebadiah Clemens – Merchant" painted on it in black letters. No sooner had the weary beasts dropped their heads when one of the doors swung open, and a stocky, middle-aged man dressed in coarse linen trousers and a sky-blue smock-coat stepped outside. Holding up the lantern he was carrying he called out in a voice infused with a broad Lincolnshire dialect.

"Lord love us Samuel Endicote what hour is this to be disturbing honest folk taking their supper?"

"And since when Zebadiah Clemens did Norton's merchants keep shopkeeper's hours?" Samuel replied as he climbed down from the wagon.

"Mercy be what a terrible thought", said Zebadiah, gripping the farmer's extended hand.

No sooner had he spoken when the other door was flung open, and four men appeared, their loose-fitting shirts tucked into the waist of their trousers, sleeves rolled up. Eager to be done for the day, working in pairs they began unloading the wagon. Carrying the heavy lengths of timber into the darkened interior of the warehouse.

"Will you and the lad join my good lady and myself at our table Samuel?"

"Thank you kindly, Zebadiah, but we've business to attend to with Minister Rathbone."

"And what of food and lodgings for the night? Only I hear tell that our parson is not as generous with his deeds as he is with his words. More especially where absentee parishioners are concerned."

Samuel stared back at him, a flicker of amusement in his eyes.

"Best you leave your warehouse door open then if what you say of his lack of hospitality is true."

"That I will. Now be off with you, my men will see to your oxen."

"And what of my furniture? Do you have what I asked for?"

"Aye, every last stick. All stored safely under my roof ready to be loaded for your return."

With that, the two men shook hands again, and with Adam following a step behind Samuel walked away down the street in search of the town's church.

To simply call it a church would be wrong as the building also served as the town's meeting-house. Being given over twice a week for religious business; on the Sabbath, and on a Thursday evening when somewhat reluctantly Minister Rathbone presided over a small congregation of pious souls whose devotion to God required a further helping of fire and brimstone. Dominating the frontage of the building was an imposing doorway with a casement window set on either side like a pair of all-seeing eyes. Although shrouded in darkness thankfully the clapperboard house alongside it, so close as to being almost joined to it, showed enough light at one of its downstairs windows to identify it. Having found his destination, approaching the front entrance, lifting the heavy brass knocker Samuel brought it down sharply against the striker plate.

In the space of a minute, the door was opened by a young girl dressed in a white linen smock-frock, a lace-edged coif framing her pallid face. Holding up the lantern she was carrying she stared up into Samuel's face. Assuming from her tightly pursed lips that it was unlikely any form of greeting would pass between them, Samuel decided to take it upon himself to initiate proceedings.

"Good evening, Missy, my name is Endicote. I'm here to see Minister Rathbone."

"You are expected sir", the young girl replied, smiling sweetly. "Kindly follow me if you will."

Retracing her steps, the maid led them along the narrow hallway. Reaching the door at the far end, after tapping gently with her knuckles she turned the handle and pushed it open.

"If you please Sir Mr. Endicote and his son are here", she announced in a timorous voice, before quickly ushering Samuel and Adam inside.

Bathed in mellow candlelight the room was rectangular in shape with dark wood paneled walls, and a white-washed plaster ceiling. Its austere interior was rescued a little by the square of red carpet, which covered most of its oak floorboards, and a framed painting of Ely Cathedral on the far wall. Standing with his back to the red-brick fireplace, warming himself in the glow from the fire was Minister Rathbone. The smoke from the long-stemmed Meerschaum pipe protruding from between his pursed lips drifting upwards and forming a blueish haze above his balding head. Although the same age as Samuel his portly figure, and soft hands showed him to be a man wholly unaccustomed to manual labor of any kind. Dressed in a long black frock coat with deep velvet cuffs, and a shirt of sheer-spun white linen with a plain wide collar, his appearance was more befitted a bishop than a parson. Suspended from a chain about his ample neck was a solid gold cross. Placing his pipe on the mantel he turned to his guests, his arms extended in a well-practiced gesture.

"Welcome! Welcome! Come seat yourselves, you must be weary after your journey."

Obediently, Samuel and Adam walked across to the two high-backed chairs placed in isolation at the center of the room.

"So, Samuel and how is life in the wilderness? " The Minister, returned to his place by the fire.

"Hard." Samuel replied. "But we are faring well. There's good timber and water, and the soil is fertile."

"And the good Lord has kept you safe from the heathen savages has he not." The clergyman's reply was intended more as a statement of fact than an inquiry.

"Aye, we are safe in God's hands", said Samuel, smarting a little at the Minister's sanctimonious remark, having more faith in a loaded musket than God's benevolence when it came to the safety of his family.

Endowing Samuel with a benevolent smile Minister Rathbone turned his gaze on Adam.

"So young Adam you wish to be wed, I trust."

But before he could finish the sentence Adam jumped to his feet.

"Pa is building us a cabin." He blurted out excitedly. "Just for Esther and me to live in."

Taken aback by the young man's outburst, the Minister's pallid face with its tracery of purple veins quickly formed itself into a frown.

Conscious of the need for the minister's consent, climbing to his feet Samuel began whispering urgently into Adam's ear. Nudging him with his elbow before returning to his chair.

"I shall be a good and dutiful husband", said Adam, having been reminded of the part he must play, his face a picture of concentration. "I, I shall take care of my new wife and see to it that no harm shall come to her. I will ... I will provide for her and not be neglectful of her needs."

"Quite so, my son. Quite so", Minister Rathbone replied not at all reassured by the young man's recited words. Unsure as to how he should respond, thankfully, before he was called upon to do so, the door opened, and carrying a heavily laden tray in her arms the young girl entered the room.

"Ah, supper!" announced the Minister, relieved by the timely distraction.

Setting the tray on the table, with the Minister's licentious gaze never leaving her the young girl began laying out its contents; a wooden board topped with a half-eaten round of cheese, a platter with cuts of cooked meat, a bowl of pickled eggs, and a basket of bread straight from the oven. She completed the setting by placing a pewter plate in front of each of the men. Conscience of her employer's unwavering gaze, with the table laid she turned and quickly left the room. Returning moments later with two leathern jacks filled with cider which she placed beside each of the two visitors. Before making her way to the head of the table, a thin-stemmed glass filled to the brim with malmsey carefully balanced on her tray. And taking care not to spill a drop of the strong, sweet wine she placed the glass in front of her employer. It was his fourth tipple since lunch so hopefully he would sleep soundly tonight, and she would be spared from his unwanted advances.

"Thank you, my child, that will be all." said the minister, eyeing the glassful of amber liquid. "Be off to your bed now. You can clear away the table in the morning."

With a bobbing curtsey, the young girl turned and hurried across the room. The wooden heels of her shoes click-clacking on the hard floor as she skirted the edges of the rich carpet before disappearing through the door.

An hour later, with the meal concluded and Adam sent to his bed, Samuel and Minister Rathbone, their features bathed in the lurid glow from the guttering candles stared at each other across the table. A half-empty decanter of ruby port occupies the space between them.

"And you are quite certain that Mistress Colwill is equally disposed to this. . . this arrangement?"

"Assuredly!" replied Samuel, putting his glass to his lips, and draining its contents in a single swallow. "Why should she not be?"

"Come now Samuel, freedom from servitude is a poor substitute for spiritual love." Rathbone replied as he reached for the decanter.

Recognizing the condescension in the Minister's response, Samuel banged the glass down hard onto the table. His face flushed from the copious amount of port he had consumed.

"She thinks it worth it. Besides Adam loves her well enough, and she is fond of the lad despite his affliction." Striking the table with his clenched fist in frustration. "She has agreed. She is for the marriage."

Wearying of the conversation, his eyes as bright as a bear, Minister Rathbone leaned forward in his chair.

"Very well. As you say it appears this arrangement has merit for both parties."

"Have you her indenture with you as I requested?" The clergyman asked, keen to have the matter resolved and to retire to his bed.

Dipping a hand into the pocket of his jerkin Samuel pulled out a folded paper. Unfolding it he placed it in the minister's proffered hand.

"And my fee?"

Removing a leather pouch from his other pocket, Samuel dropped it on the table. The unmistakable clink of coins music to the clergyman's ears. Casting his eyes over the document, Minister Rathbone quickly familiarized himself with its contents. Satisfied with its validity, holding a corner of the paper over a lighted candle, waiting until it had caught alight, he crossed to the fireplace and tossed it into the hearth. Watching as the flames quickly devoured it. The knowledge that he had rescued a child of God from a life of servitude far outweighed by the handsome ransom he had received in exchange for sanctioning her freedom.

At first light with the chill of the night still in the air Shingas, and the four Seneca warriors, their savage faces daubed with fresh war-paint emerged from the dark wall of trees. Walking in a single file they made their way towards the meadow, the damp grass shrouded in the mist rising from the stream. Splashing across to the far bank, raising his arm Shingas pointed towards the smaller of the cabins, silhouetted against the lightening sky like the upturned keel of a ship. Knowing what was expected of them, following the fence-line Tusonderongue and two other warriors slipped away. Waiting until the three warriors disappeared from view, slinging their muskets across their shoulder, Shingas and Cattawa climbed over the split-rail fence into the cornfield. Moving stealthily between the rows of maize towards the distant cabin.

At pains not to incur their father's wrath, fortified by a hearty breakfast flinging open the cabin door Saul and Joshua spilled out into the yard. Closely followed by Kit and his dog Pharaoh. Mindful of his mother's instructions, Kit began tethering the dog to the length of chain attached to the cabin wall, the hound suddenly began barking. Tugging insistently against the boy's grip on its collar in a bid to free itself. Unable to control the powerful animal, reluctantly Kit released his grip on its collar, watching enviously as the hound bounded towards the cornfield.

Alerted by the sound of barking Shingas and Cattawa stopped in their tracks. Mindful of danger, freeing his knife from its sheaf Shingas dropped down onto one knee. No sooner had Cattawa followed suit when they saw the snarling hound bounding towards them, its upper lip curled back. Teeth bared Pharaoh lunged for Shingas' throat, flecks of saliva spraying from his open jaw. Instinctively, Shingas twisted his body sideways, thrusting upwards with his knife as he did so. Plunged its naked blade deep into the dog's exposed chest. With a plaintive yelp, the stricken hound tumbled to the ground, its snarls dying away to a whimper. Its lifeblood soaked up by the freshly tilled soil. Satisfied that the animal was dead, after cleaning the blade on the animal's coat, pushing the knife into its sheath Shingas climbed to his feet.

Puzzled by Pharaoh's behavior, and wondering why the dog had suddenly stopped barking, Kit made his way towards the cornfield. Clambering up onto the split-rail fence he called out.
"Pharaoh! Here boy!" Disappointed, he called out again. "Here Pharaoh! Here boy."
"Your hound has caught a rabbit little brother", shouted Saul. "He'll not come out till he's done eating his breakfast."
Stung by his elder brother's words, Kit glared back at him angrily.
"He wouldn't do that, not my Pharaoh."
Chuckling at Kit's show of temper, with their muskets resting on their shoulder Saul and Joshua ambled away towards the sawpit.
Determined to prove Saul wrong, Kit called out again. Louder this time.
"Here Pharaoh! Here boy!"

Finally, with his patience exhausted, jumping down from the fence Kit made his way into the ripening rows of corn.

Standing barefoot on a low stool, a garland of freshly picked wildflowers fixed in her auburn hair Esther glanced down at Mrs. Endicote busy with needle and thread. Carefully tacking the hem of the long cambric dress, she was wearing. With the breakfast things still littering the table, the bed in the corner unmade, and a pair of her freshly washed bloomers airing in front of the fire Esther had never seen the room in such a mess. Time to attend to those things later Mrs. Endicote had said. Seeing that the bride-to-be was ready for her forthcoming nuptials was much more important. The decision to wear this particular dress rather than make-do with her own shabby frock had been Mrs. Endicote's idea. Determined that Esther should look the part she had insisted on it. It was a fine dress, more plain than fussy with long-fitted sleeves widening at the cuffs, and a row of matching buttons below the rounded neck. A dress she herself had worn on many occasions, not least when attending church. Though sadly given her present size it was clear to see that it was not a garment she would have further use for. With her needlework completed, gripping the edge of the table for support, Mrs. Endicote pulled herself upright. Satisfied with her work, just as she was returning the needle and thread to her sewing basket the silence was broken by the sound of musket fire.

Shocked by the sound of gunfire, quickly followed by the more terrifying sound of war-whoops, Kit stood rooted to the spot. His legs paralyzed by fear. Gripped by uncertainty, the spell was broken by the sudden appearance of two Indians moving towards him along the row of corn. The sight of their painted faces filling him with terror. With all thoughts of his hound erased from his mind turning on his heels he began racing back towards the cabin. Catching sight of the fleeing boy, tomahawk in hand, moving with the grace of a panther Cattawa lengthened his stride.

Flinging open the cabin door, with Esther a step behind her, the dress pulled up around her knees, Mrs. Endicote rushed outside.

Filled with uncertainty, the pair looked about them. Catching sight of Kit running out from the row of corn they watched in silence as he began clambering over the fence. But before the boy could haul himself over the top rail Cattawa was on him. The force of the blow from his tomahawk almost cleaving Kit's scull in two. Howling with anguish, snatching up the heavy wood-axe resting against its chopping block, with a demented scream Mrs. Endicote began running towards her son's killer. Alerted by her agonizing cry, releasing his grip on the tomahawk embedded in Kit's head, Cattawa slipped the musket off his shoulder. Resting its long barrel on the fence rail he cocked the hammer, and taking careful aim, he pulled the trigger. Watching with satisfaction as like a stricken animal Mrs. Endicote sprawled lifeless onto the ground, the axe still gripped in her hands.

With the sound of the musket ringing in her ears, Esther watched in horror as Shingas suddenly appeared at the edge of the cornfield. Terrified, with the hem of her dress still clutched in her hands she raced back towards the cabin. Catching sight of the fleeing woman, vaulting the fence with the ease of an athlete Shingas chased after her. With her heart pounding, reaching the cabin Esther dashed in through the open door, slamming it shut behind her. But just as her fingers closed around the iron bolt, the door suddenly burst inwards, the impact throwing her backwards into the room. Sprawled against the table, with a scream welling up in her throat Esther watched in horror as the figure of Shingas appeared in the doorway. Terrified, like a cornered animal she backed away from him. The palms of her hands pressed against the table for support. Stepping into the cabin, Shingas quickly scanned the room. Fearing for her life, as she edged along the table Esther's hand brushed against the discarded breadknife, her fingers instinctively closing around its handle. At least now she could defend herself. Tiring of the woman's attempt to evade him, thrusting out his hand Shingas seized Esther by the arm, pulling her towards him. With the knife gripped in her fist, raising her arm in the air Esther lunged at him, stabbing downwards at his naked chest. With contemptuous ease, reaching out his free arm Shingas grabbed her by the wrist. Slowly tightened his grip until, unable to withstand the pain, Esther uncurled her fingers, the knife slipped from her grasp and clattered onto the wooden floor. Kicking the knife aside, maintaining his hold on her wrist Shingas dragged his terrified captive out of the cabin. Fearing that at any moment she would be murdered, with a despairing cry Esther dropped to her knees.

Across from the cabin, whooping, and yelling Tusonderongue, and the two other warriors, each clutching a flaming torch came running out from the barn, closely followed by a dozen hens, flapping and squawking as they made their escape through the open doors. Inside the building, flames from the upturned barrel of tar-oil licked hungrily at the bales of hay. Opposite, the unfinished cabin was already ablaze, the bright orange flames, encouraged by the breeze running down the valley eagerly devouring its tinderbox timbers. With plumes of black smoke billowing upwards into the cloudless sky. Calling out to them, Shingas pointed towards the cabin. Eagerly the three warriors ran towards its open door and disappeared inside. Emerged moments later with their act of arson completed, and shrieking their war-cry they tossed their flaming brands onto the resin-rich shingled roof. Watching with unrestrained delight as the fire quickly took hold.

Dragging Esther up onto her feet, with flames already licking at the windows gathering his war-party around him, Shingas walked away. As they passed between the blazing buildings that had once been a barn, and her future home Esther suddenly clutched a hand to her mouth. Stifling the scream lodged in her throat at the sight of the two mutilated bodies sprawled lifelessly on the ground beside the sawpit. Pulling her by the arm Shingas made his way into the cornfield, and on into the meadow beyond. Reaching the stream, he released his grip on Esther's arm, and stepping into knee-deep water Shingas began washing the dog's blood from his hand and arm. Rooted to the spot Esther watched warily as the four young warriors began crowding around her, each studying her with child-like interest. Bolder than the others, grabbing a handful of material Cattawa attempted to lift up her skirt. Instinctively, Esther slapped his hand away. Piqued by her reaction, snatching the garland of flowers from her head the young warrior threw it onto the ground. Climbing onto the bank, Shingas glared at the young warrior.

"Enough!" The word alone enough to admonish the young warrior for his petulance. Suitably chastised, jumping into the stream Cattawa waded across to the far bank, the war party following in his wake. With no alternative other than to follow them, pulling up the hem of her dress Esther stepped into the stream. The feel of the pebbled bed on her bare feet a sudden reminder that she was not wearing any shoes. Once across, consumed by an overwhelming sense of despair, Esther looked back towards the farm. Staring forlornly at the plumes of smoke spiraling upwards from the burning buildings. A moment later, overcome with sadness, she turned away, and plagued by the scenes of horror she had witnessed Esther continued across the meadow. The same meadow where only yesterday she gathered the flowers for her garland. Her only consolation was that whatever lay ahead of her at least she was alive, and for now that was all that mattered.

With the wagon loaded with the furniture from Zebadiah Clemens' warehouse, cracking his whip Samuel urged the oxen into the river. Seated beside him on the plank of wood which served as a seat, clearly not enjoying his bumpy outing was Minister Rathbone. Ahead of them, wading through the knee-high water, eager to return to the farm, and the ceremony that lay ahead Adam suddenly stopped midstream. Shouting out he pointed an arm towards the distant column of black smoke rising above the treetops. Throwing down the whip, Samuel snatched up his musket, and calling for his son to wait he jumped down from the wagon. But Adam was already out of the river, running as fast as his leg would take him along the track towards the inky-black smudge on the canvas of blue sky.

With Minister Rathbone pulling uncertainly on the reigns the ox-wagon lumbered into the farm. Coming to an involuntary standstill when, confronted by the terrible scene before him, the clergyman allowed the thick leather straps to slip from his hands. The cluster of buildings were little more than charred skeletons, the flickering tongues of yellow and orange flames still licking at the smoldering remains of their timber walls. The roof of the main cabin had collapsed engulfing the rooms below in the smoky remains of shingles and beams. Only its impressive chimney was still standing, a tall stone obelisk among the charred and blackened timbers. Although most of the barn had been consumed by fire, miraculously the cow had somehow survived. It's calls to be milked the only semblance of normality among, the carnage. Lowering his eyes, the clergyman spotted Samuel kneeling on the ground, the body of his dead wife cradled like an infant in his arms. Beyond him draped over the fence like a discarded coat was the lifeless body of the Endicote's youngest son. Gazing out at the scene of devastation before him, he saw Adam running in from the field, his cheeks wet with tears. Clutched in his hand was a small garland of flowers. Reaching his father's side, the boy dropped onto his knees.

"Esther is gone, Pa. The savages have taken my Esther."

Hearing Adam's plaintive words, shielding his eyes from the glare of the morning sunlight Minister Rathbone looked out towards the encircling forest. Dark, and foreboding in its primitive majesty. Unconsciously, his fingers closed around the golden cross hanging about his neck, his lips moving in silent prayer. A prayer for the living. A humble petition for the safety of the young woman who had been abducted on the very day she was to be married. The dead would have their turn when he stood over them as they were lowered into the earth.

CHAPTER SEVEN

With only a narrow, unfrequented trail to guide them, the war-party and their captive moved ever deeper into the seemingly unending wilderness of mountain, and forest. An impervious wall of trunks, and boughs blanketed by a dense canopy of leafy arches. Clambering up and over the backs of wooded hills. Threading their way through tangled thickets, the air heavy with the resinous odor of pine. The occasional screech of a Red-tailed hawk the only sound. Each step taking them farther away from the frontier settlements. Without stopping for rest by mid-morning with her bare feet cut and bloodied, unable to take another step Esther dropped to her knees. Instantly Shingas was at her side, glaring down at her menacingly. Gasping for breath Esther stared up at him beseechingly. Unmoved, taking a length of rawhide rope from his carry-all, looping one end around Esther's wrist, Shingas dragged her up onto her feet, and leading her like a tethered animal he set off again but this time at a slower pace.

Thankfully, before they had travelled very far, chancing upon a fast-flowing stream Shingas called a halt. Freed of her restraint Esther stumbled towards its bank, and throwing herself onto the ground, she began gulping down handfuls of the clear, pure water. With her thirst quenched, leaning forward she plunged her head into the stream, the swiftly flowing current washing through her disheveled hair. But her respite was short-lived, eager to be on his way, taking hold of her halter Shingas set off once more. Refreshed, with water running down her neck, determined not to let the rope tighten between them hitching up her dress Esther hurried after him. Moments later, with Tusonderongue at its head, the small party was quickly swallowed up by the gloomy woods.

With darkness descending Shingas finally called a halt, and without needing a fire, finding a bed for themselves on the carpet of pine needles which covered the forest floor the four warriors were soon asleep. Following their example, with the rope removed from around her wrist Esther slumped to the ground.

Welcoming the opportunity to get a night's rest, with her head cradled in her arms she quickly drifted off into a deep sleep. Last, to find his bed, walking across to where she was lying, Shingas gazed down at the small figure curled up at his feet, the rigors of the day gone from her face. He also noticed the chafe marks on her wrists made by the rope. Promising himself that as a reward for her stoicism, tomorrow he would leave the rope in his carry-all.

Even before the first rays of sunlight had filtered through the canopy of leaves the war-party were already making their way along the narrow path as it snaked away into the encircling woods. Free of her tether, with Cattawa, and the other three warriors walking in single file behind her, matching him stride for stride Esther followed in Shinga"s wake. Although the soles of her feet were sore, and her belly ached from lack of food she felt well rested. Better yet, she had endured her first day of captivity, and although she had no idea of what ordeals lay ahead, this small accomplishment strengthened her resolve to survive.

It was still early when they came upon the cluster of wigwams. Wisps of white smoke drifting up through the smoke-hole in their roofs. It was a Wyandot village. An enemy village. A place to be avoided if they wanted to live. Alert to the danger, as they began skirting around its perimeter the silence was rudely shattered by the strident cries of a baby. Fearing that the noise would wake the camp-dogs, cocking their muskets, the war-party dropped to their knees. Their eyes alert to any signs of movement. Thankfully, much to their relief no sooner had they begun than the infant's lusty cries were swiftly silenced. Continuing on their way, within a matter of minutes they were clear of the trees, and there, stretching before them, was the reason why the Wyandots had chosen this location for their village. A vast lake, its gently rippling waters stretching away to the far horizon. Its distant shore lost against the boundless panorama of forest-covered mountains piled against the sky.

It was then that Cattawa's keen eyes spotted the cluster of birch bark canoes lying upturned on a sandy spit of land like a colony of basking seals. Eager to take advantage of their good fortune, the four young warriors dashed across towards them. Cattawa and another warrior dragged two of them down to the water's edge while Tusonderongue and the other young warrior set to work hacking at the remainder craft with their tomahawks, staving-in their birch bark sides and rendering them useless.

Seating herself between the two rowers Esther watched as Shingas climbed into the second canoe. The thought of crossing such an immense body of water in such a frail craft filling her with trepidation. With the four Seneca warriors dipping and pulling on their paddles in perfect time the two canoes moved away from the shore. Quickly gathered speed, their curved prows cutting effortlessly through the shimmering water, its surface reflecting the rays of sunlight like an upturned mirror. High above them, their wings outstretched a pair of fish-hawks circled in ever-widening spirals in the cloudless blue sky, their shrill calls echoing in the natural amphitheater.

Kneeling upright between the two rowers, thankful for the cooling breeze Esther cast a despairing look at the receding shoreline. Any hopes of rescue fading away with every stroke of the paddles. Seated in the prow of the other canoe, when they reached deeper water Shingas opened his carry-all and removed a length of fishing line with a barbed hook, and a silver lure attached to one end. Gripping the end of the line in one hand, letting it slip slowly through his fingers, Shingas lowered it into the water. The spoon-shaped lure spinning and flashing like quicksilver as it sank beneath the surface. No sooner had it disappeared, than feeling a tug on the line Shingas began hauling it in hand over hand. A shout going up from the other warriors when he pulled a large lake trout clear of the water. Dropping his wriggling catch into the bottom of the canoe, freeing the hook from its mouth Shingas cast the line over the side once more. Watching him from the other canoe, Esther stared in fascination as Shingas hauled another fish into the canoe, the water running off its scales like droplets of mercury.

With the shoreline disappearing into the distance behind them the four warriors slowed the rhythmic pace of their paddling, allowing the canoes to glide effortlessly across the glassy surface of the water with barely a ripple. Gazing across the vast lake to Esther it seemed like they were journeying across an ocean. The far shore lost somewhere beyond the horizon, and despite her dire predicament, she found herself lost in admiration at the majesty and beauty of this never-ending wilderness.

However, as the day progressed, with the sun rising higher in the cloudless sky, without any shade to protect her from its rays her enjoyment quickly waned. Her only relief coming from scooping up handfuls of water and splashing onto her exposed skin. Occasionally a warrior would pause in his paddling to dip a cupped hand into the lake and slake his thirst. With little option other than to follow their example, Esther was amazed at how pure and pleasant the water tasted.

With the golden orb of the sun slowly sinking below the peaks of the distant mountains the Seneca war-party finally reached a sandy beach on the southern shore of the lake. After dragging the canoes onto the narrow spit, eager for their supper, the warriors set to work with their knives. Gutting and cleaning the four trout that Shingas had caught. Filled with curiosity, Esther looked on, admiring the skillful way in which they went about the work. Minutes later, with their heads removed, the filleting trout, were skewered on a ramrod before being placed skin down above the glowing embers of the fire. The four young warriors crowding around like impatient children eager for the charred wood to work its magic. The aroma of roasting fish wafting up into the night air.

Hoping that one of them might take pity on her and throw her a morsel, Esther watched as the war-party feasted on the cooked fish. Tearing the flaky, white flesh from its spiny bones with their fingers, and cramming it into their mouths. But it was not to be, and having eaten their fill, wiping their oily fingers on their breechcloth the warriors moved away from the fire, and stretched out on the soft ground they quickly fell sleep.

Satisfied by the sound of their rhythmic breathing that her captors were all asleep, with hunger gnawing at her belly, on hands and knees Esther crawled tentatively towards the dying fire. The pitiful remains of the war-parties meal scattered on the ground around it. No sooner had she reached her goal when the closest to the fire lying Cattawa suddenly rolled over onto his side. Wide awake, his eyes bored into her. Hardly daring to move, Esther stared back at him, her heart racing. Slowly the seconds ticked by, and then fearing the worst, much to Esther's amazement, the young warrior simply rolled over and turned his back on her. Filled with relief, like a feral cat Esther began scavenging among the discarded fish bones for morsels of food. Savoring each scrap of flesh gleaned from the skeletons of the fish, even the pieces of charred skin. Having devoured anything edible, on hands and knees Esther returned to her sandy bed by the shore of the lake. Stretching out on her back, licking each greasy finger in turn, she stared up at the night sky, its ink-black canopy filled with the lights of distant worlds. Some shining bright, and steady like beacons of hope. Others, the more distant ones flickering like celestial fireflies. Moments later, heavy-eyed she drifted off into a deep sleep.

With the sun creeping ever higher into another cloudless blue sky, after hiding the canoes from sight, the war-party led as always by Tusonderongue left their overnight camp. Strung out in their customary single file, hugging the shoreline they moved southwards. Earlier that morning, after washing her hands and face in the lake when Esther returned to the camp, she was surprised to see each of the warriors applying fresh war-paint to his face. Although alarmed by this apparent war-like behavior, much to her surprise she found herself intrigued by the barbaric ritual. Out of curiosity, she watched as each warrior applied the coloured pigments to their face with the tip of a finger. Faithfully tracing the outline of their previous artwork. Smiling inwardly at their childlike vanity, as they passed a small mirror among them so that each warrior could admire his handiwork.

Reaching the lake's southern boundary, moving away from its shore the war-party made their way into the surrounding trees, Tusonderongue's pace lengthening with every yard. Struggled to keep up, unknown to Esther, the war-party had entered Seneca hunting grounds, the trail they were on leading them to their village. Mercifully, before her legs gave out, as they entered a small woodland clearing raising his musket Shingas fired it into the air. Whooping and yelling, the other warriors quickly followed suit, throwing up their muskets and discharging them in a ragged volley. The sound reverberating through the dark canopy of branches. Grateful for the pause in their journey, Esther dropped to her knees. But her hopes of a rest were short-lived, and eager to be on their way, taking hold of her by the arm two of the warriors began dragging her up onto her feet. Wearily Esther stared up at them, her face etched with despair. Why they had fired their muskets she had no idea, only a sense that while it might signify the end of one ordeal, it could herald the beginning of a more daunting one.

CHAPTER EIGHT

On the sloping hillside beside the village armed with a hoe Meeataho, and a group of women, some with a baby strapped to their backs moved along the rows of corn tilling the rich soil. Chattering happily amongst themselves despite the heat of the day. Occasionally erupting into fits of laughter when some intimate secret or illicit liaison was revealed. Then they heard the unmistakable crash of gunfire, rolling in like the rumble of distance thunder. Instantly, after throwing down their hoes with Meeataho racing ahead of them, shrieking like excited children the women began running towards the village.

Pushing her way through the crowd which had already gathered on the fringe of the quadrangle Meeataho watched as Shingas, his head held high came striding purposefully through the village. The four Seneca warriors, each with a bloody trophy adorning their belts following close behind. The excited crowd gathering about them clamoring for the sight of their captive. Stunned, Meeataho stared at him, her joy at the expectation of seeing him again turned to dust at the sight of the white woman walking by his side. As the war-party approached the entrance to Shingas' long-house an expectant hush settled over the jostling crowd. Sensing a change in their mood, after hesitating for a moment Shingas suddenly pulled aside the curtain, and taking hold of Esther's arm, he pushed her inside. Instantly, a great shout went up. Shingas had taken the white woman as his new wife. With his decision made, impervious to the shouts from the excited crowd, enveloped by the throng of people Shingas strode away towards the council lodge.

Standing a little way in from the doorway, disheveled and dirty from her arduous journey Esther surveyed the building's gloomy interior. A building she had never seen the like of before. Running down its center was a wide isle with what appeared to be compartments, much like the stalls in a livery stable down each side. Dotted at intervals along, its length were several fire-pits, their glowing embers giving off a mellow light. With no sign of its residents, before she had a chance to decide what to do the curtain at the doorway was suddenly pulled aside, and Meeataho stepped inside. Her jet-black eyes blazing with anger. Startled by the woman's appearance, and instantly aware of her apparent hostility, Esther backed away. With a wild cry, arms raised, her fingers hooked into talons Meeataho hurled herself towards her. Instinctively, Esther grabbed the woman's wrists, forcing her clawing fingers away from her face. Wrenching her hands free Meeataho lunged forward again. But this time Esther was ready for her, both women grabbing handfuls of each other's hair. Locked in a savage embrace they struggled back and forth neither woman willing to release their hold. Hampered by the hem of her long dress, unable to free her entangled foot, Esther stumbled backwards dragging the other woman with her. With their fingers still knotted in each other's hair, like a pair of wildcats, the two women began rolling around on the earthen floor, each struggling to straddle the other with her legs. Clawing at Esther's eyes with her free hand Meeataho managed to force her opponent onto her back. But before she could pin her rival to the ground, bending her knees, Esther lashed out with both feet, sending the young maiden sprawling backwards.

Panting with exertion, clumps of each-others hair trapped under their finger nails the two women clambered to their feet, circling each other warily. Sensing that her opponent was tiring, eager to sink her claws into Esther's face Meeataho lunged forward. Instinctively, Esther jabbed out her left arm, her tightly clenched fist striking Meeataho in the face. Stunned by the unexpected blow Meeataho staggered backwards, blood trickling from the gash in her lip. Wiping the back of her hand across her mouth, undeterred, Meeataho charged forward. Once again Esther jabbed out her left arm, her knuckles striking Meeataho's jaw, and sending her sprawling backwards onto the ground. With her arms hanging passively at her side Esther stared down at the young Indian woman, hoping she had knocked the fight out of her. Dazed by the force of the blow, Meeataho looked up at her, puzzled as to why the woman had not continued her attack. Encouraged by her apparent stupidity Meeataho climbed slowly to her feet, and tossing back her mane of black hair, she reached for the knife strapped to her belt. Horrified, Esther backed away, frantically looking around her for a way of escape. With her rival now at her mercy, Meeataho edged forward, forcing Esther back towards the wall of the long-house, her knife gripped in her hand. Helpless, her fists little help against the blade of a knife Esther awaited her fate. Knowing that her adversary was trapped, with a wild shout Meeataho raised the knife into the air. But before she could strike, a sudden pain lanced through her shoulder. Instinctively, Meeataho turned around, staring in disbelief as the old woman lashed out again with the hoe, bringing it down on her upraised arm. The force of the blow knocking the knife from the Meeataho's grip. Not content with disarming the young maiden, the old woman raised the hoe above her head. Cackled with laughter as she watched Meeataho fleeing towards the doorway. With the attacker gone, setting down her hoe the old woman turned to Esther, her broad smile revealing a mouthful of decaying teeth. Clearly impressed by Esther's fighting skills, holding up her bony arms, with her fists clenched the old woman began jabbing out with her left arm, mimicking Esther's actions, the smile never leaving her face.

As she watched the old woman's antics Esther suddenly found herself transported back in time to the interior of a large Suffolk barn. Perched high up on one of the huge crossbeams, which supported its cavernous, pitched roof, giving her a bird's eye view of the ground below her. At the center of the barn was a small roped-off square no bigger than a small room. Surrounding it was a dense crowd of men, cheering and baying like a pack of blood hounds. Confined inside the ropes, stripped to the waist two bare-knuckle fighters stood toe to toe trading blow after sickening blow. Neither man willing to give an inch. Their muscular bodies glistening with sweat. Their open mouth's dragging in lungsful of air. Their faces and fists bearing the scars of combat. One of them, the older of the two fighters, was her father. A broad-shouldered man with narrow hips, and hands the size of sledgehammers. His opponent was much younger, and despite the bloody swelling around his eyes where her father's brine-soaked fists had pummeled them until they were almost shut, he was also very handsome. Both fascinated and disgusted by the spectacle, she found herself unable to leave. Unwilling to even look away despite the revulsion she felt until it had finally ended. She also remembered with equal clarity how later that same night, with the blood washed from the cuts around his eyes, a clean blue linen shirt covering his muscular torso, the young fighter had carried her back to the same barn. Remembering how he had held her in his strong arms. The tenderness of his touch as he gently caressed her face, her neck and her breasts with his calloused hands. And although not yet sixteen, on that warm summer night, she had known a man for the first time.

Returned to the present by the sound of the old woman's jabbering voice, Esther stared at her. She was obviously trying to tell her something, but Esther had no idea what it was. Frustrated by Esther's lack of understanding of what she was saying, grabbing hold of her by the wrist, the old woman pulled her over to where a large cooking-pot was suspended over a low fire. Its contents: a kind of porridge made from boiled maize flavored with berries and pumpkin seeds gently simmering away. Taking hold of the swan-necked ladle, a prized procession plundered from some settlement kitchen, anchored in the gluttonous substance the old woman began stirring. Agitating the solidified mass until she was satisfied with its consistency. Once this had been achieved, ladling a generous helping into an earthenware bowl she handed it to Esther. Watching intently as the Yengeese woman lifted the bowl to her lips, and using her two fingers began scooping the porridge into her mouth. The ladle already filled with a second helping should it be needed.

Finally, unable to cram anymore of the porridge into her mouth smiling her thanks Esther placed the empty bowl on the ground. With her ward suitably nourished, dropping the ladle back into the pot, gesturing for Esther to follow her the old woman made her way along the narrow aisle. Stopping halfway along, pointing with a spindly finger at the entrance to one of the partitioned rooms, she ushered Esther inside.

To Esther's surprise, while it appeared quite small from the outside, inside the room was surprisingly spacious. Separating it from the apartments on either side were high wooden partitions, giving the interior a degree of privacy. The dirt floor was covered in strips of rush matting, with some wicker baskets, and a collection of earthenware pots stacked up against the wall. The room's only furniture where a pair of cots each just wide enough to accommodate two people, both of them half-hidden under a pile of animal furs. After taking a moment to survey her new surroundings, when she turned around much to her surprise Esther found that the old woman had disappeared. Finding herself alone for the first time since her abduction, overwhelmed by events, and exhausted from the rigors of her journey, slumping down onto one of the cots, with her head cradled in the crook of her arm Esther prayed for sleep to come to her rescue. To free her, if only for a few precious moments from this living nightmare.

Having had her prayer answered, Esther was awoken by the sound of voices, and just for a minute, she was gripped by a feeling of hope. But her optimism was quickly extinguished when she recognized the unfamiliar language they were conversing in. With the reality of her situation reaffirmed, unable to contain her curiosity she climbed off the cot, and pulling aside the curtain covering the narrow doorway Esther peered outside. Watching as groups of people, mainly women, and young children began making their way to their respective compartments. Many of them, especially the children, stealing a furtive glance in her direction as they passed bye before quickly looking away. Two of the bolder ones, a boy and a girl staring back at her with mischievous curiosity before scampering away at the sound of their mother's voice. Alone once more, settling back onto the cot the melodious harmony of hushed voices acting like a lullaby Esther closed her eyes. Desperately hoping that the one who had claimed her for his own would not be returning.

This time it was someone shaking her, which woke her, and looking up Esther saw the figure of the old woman standing over her. A pair of beaded moccasins in one of her bony hands, and what looked like a pole in the other. Filled with apprehension, Esther climbed to her feet, and without saying a word throwing the moccasins onto the cot, the old woman thrust the pole into Esther's hand. Quickly realizing that what she was holding was a hoe, putting it to one side Esther began pulling on the moccasins, amazed at how well they fitted. Happy with her new footwear, retrieving the hoe she hurried after the old woman. Falling in beside her as she made her way through the waking village.

When the pair reached the fields on the outskirts of the village a dozen or so women were already at work. Chattering happily among themselves as they moved slowly along the rows of ripening corn, busy with their hoes. Some had a baby strapped to their backs, their chubby faces smeared with bear oil, their enormous coal black eyes staring out at everything around them with innocent curiosity. With her spirits lifted by the idyllic scene, a stern look from the old woman quickly reminded Esther that the reason she was here was to work. Selecting an untended row, hoe in hand Esther began working it into the rich soil, her mind focused on the work. Enjoying the distraction which it provided. Occasionally, when she straightened up to stretch her back, she would catch sight of an inquisitive glance in her direction. The culprit quickly averted her eyes when she saw that Esther had noticed her. As the morning wore on, having become accustomed to her presence, these moments became fewer, and when she did happen to meet another woman's gaze more often than not, they would exchange a smile.

With their work in the cornfield finished the group of women began moving lower down the hillside to an area of open ground planted with squash and pumpkin. Before following them, desperate to relieve herself, Esther lingered behind, and with no bloomers to contend with she quickly emptied her bladder onto the dry ground. Re-joining the group of women, unbuttoning the neck of her dress Esther began working away with her hoe. The old woman never far away, a constant chaperone.

It was the sound of a child's voice which caused Esther to straighten up, and brushing back her hair she was amazed to see a young girl running across the field towards her. At first glance, she looked to be about seven or eight, and judging by the paleness of her skin, and the full-length linen dress she was wearing she was certainly not an Indian child. The next thing Esther knew was that the child's skinny arms were wrapped tightly around her legs, her pitiful voice pleading with her. Gazing down at the girl's upturned face, although she couldn't understand what the girl was saying Esther immediately recognized the langue as French. Dropping onto one knee she took the young girl into her arms.
"There, there now, don't be afraid."
Around them an expectant hush suddenly settled over the watching women, and looking over the young girl's shoulder Esther saw why.

Striding purposefully towards them, her face set into a scowl was a stockily built woman with muscular arms. Sensing an imminent confrontation pushing herself up onto her feet, Esther instinctively clenched her hands into fists. Free from Esther's embrace, clearly terrified by the sight of the approaching woman, clutching onto Esther's dress the young girl sought sanctuary behind her legs. With less than a yard between them, the woman stared into Esther's face, shouting at her in a guttural voice. Although she couldn't understand what she was saying, it was clear to Esther that she was demanding the return of the child. Reluctant to comply with her demand, tight-lipped she stared back at her. After receiving no response, with an angry cry the burly woman made a grab for the child. Instinctively, Esther took a step back, and stooping down she retrieved her Hoe. Again, the burley woman voiced her demand. Jabbing a finger at the young girl peering out at her from behind Esther's skirts. Slowly Esther shook her head. No! Incensed by Esther's reaction, with her arms outstretched the woman lunged forward. Immediately, Esther raised her hoe, in the air. Shocked by the threatening gesture the woman stepped back. Angry but also a little uncertain. Half-shocked, half-excited, fully expecting that at any moment the two women would begin fighting over the child the onlookers formed themselves into a circle around them.

It was then that the old squaw intervened. Pushing her way through the ring of women she positioned herself between the two antagonists. Seeing herself as a mediator in the matter she turned to Esther, pointing a finger at the locket hanging on a silver chain around her neck. Gesturing for her to remove it. Instinctively, Esther placed a protective hand over the locket. Shaking her head as she did so. The locket had once belonged to her mother, a woman she could barely recall, and for that reason alone she was loathed to give it up. Sensing her reluctance, the old woman pointed at the locket again. More insistent this time. Speaking to Esther as she did so, her tone of voice making it quite evident that she was being scolded for her reluctance to part with the trinket. Plagued by indecision, staring down at the young girl's wretched face Esther's resolve weakened, and releasing her grip on the hoe, she removed the locket from around her neck.

Gripping the silver chain between thumb, and finger the old woman dangled it enticingly in front of the burly woman. Her words extolled its virtues as an amulet against sickness, and witchcraft with the persuasiveness of a snake-oil salesman. Eventually, convinced by the old woman's rhetoric, snatching the locket from her the burly woman slipped it into the small pouch hanging from her belt. Immediately, a sigh went up from the watching crowd. The tension evaporating like a morning mist, and seemingly quite happy to have exchanged a child for a trinket, with a shrug of her shoulders the burley woman made her way back across the field.

With the woman gone, kneeling in front of the young girl Esther looked into the child's face.
"What is your name?"
Instantly the girl's face dropped.

Sensing her disquiet, reaching out Esther took hold of one of the child's hands. "Don't be afraid."

Immediately the young girl's body stiffened. Her crumpled face threatening to burst into floods of tears at any moment.

"Elle est Francaise! Francais!" She is French! French! Shouted the old woman pointing at the young girl. A language she had learned from a Jesuit priest who had once resided in her village when she was a young girl herself.

Although the words themselves were unfamiliar, it was clear to Esther that she was telling her that the young girl was French. A child from a country England had been at war with for as long as Esther could remember. But here none of that mattered. Like herself, she was a captive of these savage people, and because of this, there was already a kind of kinship between them. A bond formed as much by their circumstances as by the color of their skin. So, smiling brightly, reaching out Esther took the young girl into her arms, hugging her to her. For better or worse, whether as a younger sister or an adopted child, she was to be her responsibility now. Someone she must care for as if she were her own. Looking on, her face creased into a rare smile the old woman slowly nodded her head. Having been without any close family of her own for so long, not only did she have a new daughter-in-law but now it seemed she had also acquired a granddaughter.

The next morning saw them back in the fields once more. Esther, busy with her hoe. The French girl following her like a shadow. The previous evening, they had both made an attempt to improve their appearance. Armed with a porcupine comb, ignoring the child's howls of protest, Esther had set about freeing the tangles from her shoulder-length hair. She had wanted to put it into a plait but after deciding her new charge had endured enough for one evening she applied a small amount of bear grease instead. Working it into the child's mane of hair with her fingers until it shone like strands of copper wire. The transformation was completed by a scrub with a wet cloth, revealing a round sunburnt face with a pert little nose, and butterfly lips as pink as a wild rose. Esther had also used the comb on her matted hair and done her best to repair the tears in her dress. The whole process watched over by the old squaw, hovering over them like a schoolmistress. Pointing every-now-and then at a missed tangle or a tear not stitched together to her liking.

It was late morning when the group of young children made their way onto the strip of open ground running alongside the cornfield. Dividing themselves into two teams, using a ball the size of a baby's head made from animal skins, a game of "Catch, and keep" was soon underway. The players of one team passed the ball to each other while the opposing team did all it could to steal it from them. Suddenly a pass was dropped, and in an instant, shrieking with excitement, players from both teams threw themselves onto the ground, each scrambling to retrieve the ball. Standing apart from the melee, a young girl spotted the French girl watching them and waving her arm she beckoned to her. Unsure, the French girl moved closer to Esther, her hand clutching at her dress. It seemed she was not confident enough to let go of her new mother's apron strings just yet. Sensing her reluctance, with a shrug of her shoulders the Seneca girl turned away. Having witnessed the incident, Esther placed her hand on the young girl's head, stroking her hair reassuringly. Given time she knew the shyness would pass. Turning her back on the rough and tumble game Esther caught sight of a young mother with a baby strapped to her back on a cradleboard looking across at her. Instinctively, Esther smiled at her, watching delightedly when the young woman smiled back at her. She was accepted.

Even before her feet touched the rush mat floor Esther knew her period had started. Although she was usually aware of their timing, with all that had happened she had given little thought to such things. Reluctantly, gritting her teeth she pulled herself upright, grimacing at the pain in her groin. Standing watching her, impatient to be off, taking hold of Esther's hand, the French girl began pulling her towards the aisle. Unsure of what she should do Esther hesitated, gripping the corner post for support as another sharp pain knifed through her lower abdomen. She wanted to tell the girl to wait but knew she wouldn't understand if she did. Then quite suddenly, like a genie from a bottle the old woman appeared in front of her. Sensing something was wrong she stared at Esther with hooded eyes. Watching knowingly as Esther winced with pain. Seeking confirmation, pulling up the hem of Esther's dress the old woman peered up between Esther's legs. Filled with embarrassment, Esther stared down at her cheeks flushed with color. Releasing her hold on the dress, quick as a cat the old woman was gone. Returning a few moments later, clutching a trade blanket in her hand, taking hold of Esther by the wrist she pulled her into the aisle. Once outside the long-house, with an agility that belied her age, Esther's wrist still firmly gripped in her hand, ignoring the stares from the women making their way to the fields the old woman hurried through the village. The French girl scampering along behind them like an excited puppy, totally oblivious to what was happening.

Sited well away from the other long-houses although slightly smaller in size than its neighbors, it was its isolated location rather than its appearance which hinted at the building's purpose. Approaching the doorway the old woman released her grip on Esther's wrist, and thrusting the blanket into her hand, pulling aside the curtain she pushed Esther inside. Eager to follow her guardian inside, the old woman grabbed the young girl by the arm and pulled her away.

"Pour Femme! Pour Femme! For women! For women! "Pas d'enfants! No children!" Repeating the words several times until eventually, the child understood what she was saying.

Even before her eyes had become accustomed to the building's gloomy interior Esther's nostrils were immediately assailed by the overwhelming stench of unwashed bodies. A veritable cocktail of rancid odors hanging in the air like an invisible mist. Puzzled at first as to why the old woman had brought her here, as Esther looked around the building it soon became obvious to her. Her condition confirming the building's real purpose, and while she struggled to understand why women should be treated in this way, surprisingly she was not appalled by it. Unlike her accommodation, the building comprised a large single room without divisions or compartments. The only natural light entering through a single smoke-hole in the over-arching roof directly above a central fire-pit. Lining three of the walls were rows of low cots most of which were occupied by women in various stages of undress. Each with a blanket pressed between their thighs. Strangest of all was that despite the lack of privacy there was a distinct feeling of intimacy among its inhabitants.

It was then that her gaze was drawn towards the group of women squatting on rush mats around the fire. The clouds of sweet-scented smoke emanating from their short-stemmed pipes helping to mask the impurities seeping from their pores. Each of them was listening intently as a buxom woman, the top of her doeskin dress pulled down, began recounting the intimate details of a recent sexual liaison. Becoming aware of Esther's presence, pausing in her story-telling the woman turned and stared at the newcomer. Immediately, filled with curiosity, the other inmates followed suit, their eyes taking in every detail. Eventually, losing interest in the new arrival the buxom woman returned to her story. Concluding the licentious tale by holding up her little finger, while at the same time pouting her lips to show her disappointment. With her audience shrieking with laughter, taking advantage of the distraction Esther moved across to one of the cots. Finding a vacant spot alongside two young maidens huddled together like Siamese twins, lifting the front of her dress Ester pushed the blanket up between her thighs.

By the third day, despite its squalid conditions Esther's appreciation of the building and its function was complete. While not particularly pleasant at least it gave the inmates a chance to escape from the everyday tasks which were a woman's lot. Food and drink were brought to them daily, with nothing more expected of them other than to idle away their time until their menstruations had ended. Having been befriended by an older woman even the two teenagers seemed happier. Spending much of their time decorating a leather pouch with colored beads, and lengths of porcupine quills that the old woman had given them.

With the upper half of her dress pulled down around her waist, her face, arms and small rounded breasts glistening with sweat, intrigued by the game being played amongst the women, Esther crossed to the fire-pit. Seating herself cross-legged on one of the rush mats, her elbows on her knees, chin resting between her outstretched fingers, totally absorbed she watched the two women competing against one another. Quietly studying the rudiments of the game. Observing the tactics, and sleight-of-hand used by each player to outwit her opponent.

The game began with both players in possession of three disc-shaped markers made from hardened clay, the size of a pigeon's egg. With their markers clutched in one hand, on a signal from the buxom woman both players clapped their hands together and clenching them into fists they hid them behind their backs. As she had issued the challenge the buxom woman then began moving the markers from one hand to another into her desired sequence; a single marker in one hand, and two markers in the other, or all three markers in one hand, the other left empty. Satisfied with her choice, with her fists clenched she brought them round again, holding them out in front of her. Silently, the other woman began scrutinizing the buxom woman's clenched fists, searching for a clue as to what she had concealed in each of her hands. Having reached her decision, moving her own discs into position she brought her hands out from behind her back. Poker-faced the two women stared across at each other then, with a shout both women opened their hands. A cry going up from the onlookers, the buxom woman had outfoxed her opponent again and won the game.

Disgruntled, the loser climbed to her feet, and throwing down her markers, she walked away. Scooped up the small pile of beads, her winnings from the game, the buxom woman began scanning the faces of the audience seated around the fire in search of another opponent. Fixing her gaze at Esther she pointed a finger at the discarded markers, inviting her to pick them up. Intrigued by the challenge other women began crowding around the fire. Watching with mounting interest as Esther picked up the three discarded markers. The challenge had been accepted. Filled with confidence the buxom woman jabbed out a finger, pointing at the buttons on Esther's dress. Identifying them as acceptable to her as Esther's wager. With little else to offer, fingering each of the four pearl buttons in turn Esther nodded her head in agreement. With the bet agreed, placing the pile of beads she had just won onto the mat beside her the buxom woman slowly nodded her head. Let the game begin.

With her three markers gripped in her hand, on the signal from her opponent, with her hands clenched into fists Esther hid them behind her back. The two contestants stared at one another across the glowing embers of the fire. Gathered around them, the small crowd of women looking on with bated breath. Then in one flowing movement, with a disdainful smile, the buxom woman brought her hands around in front of her. Ignoring her scornful look, Esther focused her attention on the woman's clenched fists. Although the size of the woman's hands put her at an advantage, Esther was equally aware that cunning and subterfuge also played their part in the game. It was then that she observed the slight relaxation of the woman's right hand, the same ploy she had used against her last opponent. Suspecting that the woman meant to embarrass her by using the same trick, Esther decided to call her bluff, and bringing her own hands into view she uncurled her fingers. Instantly a shout went up from the onlookers, Esther had matched the woman's challenge. Outsmarted, by her opponent, nodding her head in acknowledgement the burley woman threw a brightly colored bead onto the mat. Now it was Easter's turn.

The next evening, with their periods over taking advantage of the gathering darkness Esther and two other women slipped out of the menstruation lodge. With her companions leading the way, skirting the outlying long-houses the three women made their way along the banks of the meandering stream. Reaching a spot where the purling waters had formed a deep pool close to the bank, dropping to their knees the three women immersed their blood-stained blankets in the water. Scrubbing them against the stream's pebbled bed, the darkening wavelets carrying away the evidence of their involvement in the women's confinement.

With the blanket purged of all traces of her blood, Esther made her way to the long-house which had now become her home. Stepping inside she was immediately enveloped in the warmth from the cooking fires dotted at intervals along the central isle. The rows of ripened corn hanging from the rafters glowing like gold in their flickering firelight. The welcoming murmur of voices coming from the apartments as families enjoyed their evening meal. The hushed tones of a mother singing a lullaby to her tired child all adding to the sense of harmony. Then suddenly a joyful cry rang out, and smiling from ear to ear the French girl came running down the aisle towards her, flinging her arms around Esther's legs, clinging to them like a limpet. Stooping down, Esther took the young girl into her arms, hugging her tightly to her chest. Amazed at how overjoyed she was to be reunited with the child. Freeing herself from the child's grip, Esther looked up to see the old woman hovering over them. Staring at her with her piercing, coal-black eyes. Mindful that she was still holding the damp blanket, muttering her thanks Esther held it out in front of her. Instantly, the old woman snatched it from her, running her eyes over Esther as she did so. Tut-tutting through blackened teeth at her disheveled appearance, and the filthy state of her dress. Blushing with embarrassment, Esther instinctively tugged at the buttonless neck of her dress with her fingers; her auspicious start had not lasted long.

Muttering something un-comprehensible under her breath, the old woman hurried away. Disappearing into one of the rooms she emerged moments later with a doeskin dress draped over her arm, its neck and sleeves beautifully decorated with colored beads. Walking up to Esther, her face devoid of expression she held it out in front of her. Quickly realizing that the dress was for her, smiling in gratitude while reaching out Esther took it from her. Amazed at how soft and light it felt in her hand. No sooner had she taken possession of her new dress when the curtain was pulled aside, and there standing in the doorway was the tall figure of Shingas.

Shocked by his sudden appearance; this was the first time she had seen him since he had brought her to the village, clutching the dress to her chest Esther shrank away from him. Expressionless, Shingas stared at her for a moment, then turning his gaze on the French girl he said something to the old woman. A hard edge to his voice. With a haughty tilt of her chin, the old woman stared back at him defiantly. Replying in a strong voice, her words imbued with matriarchal authority. Although ignorant of what had passed between them, judging from how the old woman had demonstrated her authority Esther wondered if the pair might be related, a mother and son perhaps? No sooner had the thought struck her when, taking hold of Esther's arm in a grip that made her wince the old woman began leading her away.

Watching as the two women moved away, after hesitating for a moment, crouching down Shingas looked into the face of the young French girl, a benign expression on his save features. Finding himself rewarded with a small smile, turning away Shingas made his way along the empty isle. The young girl followed a step behind him. Entering his compartment, he seated himself on one of the low cots gesturing to the young girl to follow suit. No sooner where the pair settled, when Esther returned carrying a crude trencher filled with food, strips of roasted meat still hot from the fire, boiled ears of corn and a flat loaf of unleavened bread. Placing the wooden dish at Shingas' feet, stepping back she watched nervously as he began scrutinizing the meal. Satisfied with her offering, picking up a piece of freshly cooked meat Shingas pointed towards the other cot. Obediently, Esther took her place beside the young girl, her eyes fixed on the savage warrior seated opposite her. Conscious of her attention, wiping the back of his hand across his mouth Shingas nodded towards the trencher of food. Relieved that they were to be included in the meal, selecting a few morsels of meat she handed them to the French girl along with an ear of corn. Smiling as she began wolfing down the food. Having attended to her charge, with her stomach rumbling with hunger, tearing off a corner of the loaf Esther helped herself to what remained of the meat. Outside, standing unnoticed in the shadowy isle the old woman peered in on the scene of domesticity. A satisfied smile spread across her wrinkled face.

Late into the night, satisfied that Shingas was lost in a deep sleep, carefully removing the French girl's arm from around her neck, with the doeskin dress clutched under her arm Esther slipped out of the cot. Leaving the small compartment, guided more by memory than light, she made her way to the doorway, and pulling aside the curtain she stepped outside into the moonlit night. Taking the path which had now become familiar to her, Esther hurried through the cluster of long-houses. Once clear of the village, reaching the edge of the cornfield she made her way down the gently sloping hillside towards the stream. The ever-changing sound of its purling waters carried up to her by the warm, gentle breeze.

Quickening her pace, in seconds Esther reached its grassy bank. The swirling current running deep and fast as it snaked its way around the base of the hill. It's rippling surface flowing like quicksilver. Placing the doeskin dress on the bank, grasping the hem of her dress with both hands she pulled it up over her head. Bathed in moonlight, Esther gazed down at her naked body, amazed by the whiteness of her skin in contrast to her sunburned arms. Then, with the dress clutched tightly in her hand she walked into the stream, wading tentatively through the swirling water, her feet feeling for a footing on the smooth pebbles. Reaching mid-stream, with the water at waist height taking a deep breath Esther slowly lowered herself into the stream. Deeper, and deeper until all that was visible were the long amber tresses of her hair snaking out in the current like silken threads of eelgrass. Surfacing, she gulped in a mouthful of air before immersing herself once more. Thrusting up to the surface again moments later, her mouth opened, gasping for breath. Exhilarated she pushed back the strands of wet hair from her face.

It was then that she saw him standing at the water's edge, his unblinking gaze fixed on her naked body. Instinctively Esther clutched the dress to her breasts, concealing her nakedness. But it was a forlorn gesture, and stepping into the stream Shingas began wading towards her. His chiseled features as imperturbable as ever. The desire in his hooded eyes was unmistakable. Terrified, Esther backed away the dress still pressed against her chest, her other arm extended out in front of her. Her palm held up like a shield. With the waters swirling around her she watched in horror as Shingas closed the gap between them. Despairingly she looked towards the fair bank. So near, and yet so far away.

But it was already too late and grabbing her by the arm Shingas began dragging her across the stream. Esther wanted to shout out. A cry for help no matter how futile but the words died in her throat. Strangled by fear. Near the bank Esther suddenly felt her feet slipping from under her, and losing her balance, arms outstretched she fell headlong into the water. Watching despairingly as the capricious stream snatched the dress from her fingers, carrying it off dipping, and dancing into the darkness. Tearing her eyes away, rolling over onto her back Esther gazed up at the figure of Shingas towering over her, tall and menacing. Instinctively, she lashed out at him with her legs, her face contorted with anger. Brushing her flailing limbs aside with his arm, dropping to his knees Shingas forced her over onto her stomach and placing both his hands against her back, he pushed her face-down into the water. With his quarry subdued, grabbing hold of each of Esther's legs Shingas wrenched them apart, pushing forward at the same time, forcing her up onto her knees. Lifting her head clear of the water, sensing his intention with both her arms free Esther lunged forward. Her fingers clawed at the grassy bank for a hand-hold. Instantly a searing pain burned through her scalp as Shingas grabbed a handful of her hair. Wrenching her head back until she thought her neck would break. Subdued and helpless like a tethered animal, Esther endured his urgent, ever-quickening thrusts in silence. Numbing her mind as he took his pleasure. Thankful that at least she was spared the sight of his terrifying face. Silently willing the defilement of her body to end. Mercifully, her ordeal was soon over, and falling back onto his heels, open-mouthed, his chest heaving Shingas released his grip on her hair.

On all fours, hardly daring to move, not even to turn her head Esther listened as Shingas splashed his way across to the opposite bank. Waiting until all she could hear was the tranquil babbling of the stream, satisfied that he had gone, she pushed herself up onto her knees. Instinctively, she reached between her thighs, her fingers brushing over the soft bush of pubic hair, sticky with his seed. Filled with disgust, climbing unsteadily to her feet Esther waded out of the shallows into deeper water, and with the currant swirling around her legs, she gently lowered herself into the stream. Her back resting on its pebbled bed, arms and legs spread out like the points of a star. Holding her face above the rippling surface Esther stared up at the moon-lit sky. Silently praying that the crystal-clear waters flowing between her open legs would cleanse and purify her.

The next morning, wearing her new doeskin dress, grim-faced Esther made her way to the fields. Staring straight ahead, ignoring the admiring glances of the other women, she lengthened her stride. Walking alongside her, sensing something was amiss the French girl glanced up occasionally to see if Esther's expression had softened. Only to find herself disappointed. When they eventually reached the cornfield, spotting a group of children playing a game with wooden hoops, eager to leave her grumpy companion, the young girl scampered away. Watching as her charge joined in the game, pleased to be left alone Esther set about her work. Driving her hoe into the hard ground as if she were chopping the head off a snake. Oblivious to the chattering of the women working alongside her.

No sooner had Esther reached the end of the row when a sudden commotion at the far side of the cornfield caught her attention. Turning to see what had caused it, she was surprised to see several women come running out from between the rows of corn as though they were being chased by the devil himself. Puzzled by their behavior, the next thing she knew a horse galloped into view, coming to a halt at the edge of the cornfield. Its body trembling, its eyes wide with fear. Stunned by the animal's sudden appearance, after overcoming her initial surprise, laying her hoe on the ground Esther began slowly walking towards the frightened animal, talking to it as she drew closer, her voice calm and reassuring.

Meanwhile, alerted by the terrified cries of the women Pahotan, and a handful of warriors began running out from the village. Catching sight of the trader's horse they instantly recognized it as the animal which had carried the dead warrior back to the village. Having no use for the animal themselves, yet reluctant to kill the creature they had simply driven the horse into the forest. An easy meal for a pack of wolves or a bear perhaps. Yet amazingly here it was, half-starved but alive. Pushing aside his prior reluctance, with his decision made, turning to one of the warriors Pahotan gestured for him to hand him his musket. Taking the firearm from him, he called out a warning to Esther.

Distracted by the sound of the warrior's voice, turning her head Esther watched in horror as Pahotan raised his musket. Quickly interposing herself between Pahotan and the horse she called out imploringly.
"No! Don't shoot! Please don't shoot." Her arms held out in front of her defensively.
Startled by the woman's reaction Pahotan lowered the barrel of the musket. Although he couldn't understand what the white woman was saying, it was plain by her actions that she was shielding the animal. Encouraged by the stay of execution, crossing to the freshly harvested heap of ripened corn, picking up an ear, she began walking towards the horse. Uncertain, the horse shied away. Nervously pawing at the ground with a front hoof. Instantly, Esther stopped in her tracks, her fingers busy stripping away the dry husk. Waiting until the horse had settled, she moved forward again. Talking softly as she edged closer, her voice calm, reassuring. The ear of corn held out in front of her invitingly. With hunger prevailing, stretching out its neck the starving animal took the offering of food from her hand. Grinding the maize between its blackened teeth. With the animal distracted, Esther began running her eyes over the horse's emaciated body. Saddened at the sight of its ribs protruding from its mangy coat like the skeleton of a ship. Having won the animal's trust, as she contemplated what

she should do next, Esther suddenly caught sight of the young French girl walking towards the horse chattering away in her native tongue, her small, outstretched hands filled with corn. A smile illuminating her sunburnt face as the animal began eating the offering of golden seeds.

Looking on, angered at being made to look the fool, shouting something contemptible Pahotan sent the watching women scurrying back into the cornfield. Having done all she could to prove how harmless the creature was, hoping that he had got the message Esther turned towards him. Glaring back at her, filled with admiration at the child's boldness Pahotan slowly nodded his head, and handing the musket to the warrior he had taken it from, turning away he began making his way back towards the village.

It didn't take long before news of the horse's arrival, and the bravery of the young girl spread like wildfire through the village. Her actions quickly dispelling any fears the people might have harbored over the presence of the animal in the village. The moment the horse had taken the corn from her outstretched hand Esther knew that the animal could hold the key to their salvation, a chance to escape from captivity, not just for herself but for the girl too. For she could no sooner leave her behind than she could her own daughter or sister. And so, with the idea firmly planted in her mind, knowing that given the poor condition the horse was in any attempt at escaping now would be madness, Esther knew her first task lay in improving the animal's health.

But first, there was the problem of where to keep it. For while most had accepted the animal, Esther knew that she couldn't just allow it to wander about the village. So, with help from the young girl and, the old woman she set about constructing a corral at the edge of the village. A wooden enclosure constructed from upright posts driven into the ground, and interwoven with branches, large enough to accommodate the horse. Given its relative flimsiness, as an added precaution against the animal escaping, Esther also secured its front legs with a rawhide hobble. With this task completed a regular feeding regime was put in place consisting of a plentiful supply of dried grass supplemented by a helping of corn, which Esther boiled and pulped into a mash; a mixture farmer Endicote had fed to their cow when its milk had dried up. Esther also discovered that as well as its cosmetic qualities, a liberal amount of bear grease applied as a salve to the horse coat was also an effective cure for mange.

With the animal's condition improving day by day, to ensure the young mare's survival, and with it their hopes of escape Esther knew she must prove its usefulness, in particular to the women of the village. Well aware that if she didn't, when winter came and the hunting was bad, to feed their families many of them would not hesitate to reach for their knives. Esther didn't have to wait long for an answer to present itself. Her eureka moment came the very next afternoon as she watched a group of women returning from the forest laden down with wood for their fires. Next morning, eager to put her plan into action, while most of its occupants were still asleep in their beds, creeping out of the long-house Esther and the young girl made their way to the corral. After feeding the hungry animal a handful of corn, slipping the halter the old woman had crafted from strips of rawhide over its head, the pair led the horse into the surrounding woods. Several hours later, with the horse laden down with firewood they returned to the village. The looks of delight on the faces of the watching woman at having been relieved of this time-consuming labor adequate proof that the last thing they would want was for the animal to be butchered. So, with the horse's safety secured, each morning Esther, accompanied by the young French girl would venture into the forest, there comings and goings accepted as a part of the everyday life of the village.

One afternoon, returning from the forest as the pair began unloading the wood they had collected, stacking it in a pile at the edge of the quadrangle, Esther noticed that they had attracted an audience. With the last log thrown onto the woodpile turning to the small group of watching children, with a wave of her arm Esther beckoned to them. Instantly the children, boys and girls came rushing across to her, shrieking with excitement as she lifted each of them onto the horse's back. Taking up the lead-rope, with the rider's clinging to each other like a troop of monkeys Esther began leading the horse between the rows of long-houses. The children's mothers looking on with smiling faces.

Approaching the outskirts of the village Esther's gaze was drawn towards a group of older boys and girls standing on a patch of open ground facing each other in two rows separated by a narrow gap. She also noticed that most of them, including the girls, had a stick clutched in their hands. Intrigued, as she looked at a boy who had been standing off to one side suddenly began sprinting towards them. No sooner had he entered the lane formed by the two ranks of children when then began lashing out, striking him with their clenched fists and sticks. Shrieking out loud as they delivered their blows. Dismayed, clutching her hand to her mouth Esther watched as he staggered under the barrage of blows raining down on him from all sides. A sigh of relief escaping her lips as regaining his momentum he stumbled on. Emerging bloodied but triumphant from the gauntlet. Instantly, whooping with delight, the ranks of children quickly crowded around him, lifting the triumphant boy high into the air. Filled with a sense of unease by the spectacle, pulling on the lead-rope Esther continued on her way to the stream. The sound of the children's jubilant voices gradually fading away.

Standing knee-deep in the water, as the horse slaked its thirst, filled with a sudden taste for mischief, Esther began scooping up handfuls of water and splashing the children sitting astride the horse's back. Laughing out loud as they howled in protest. On the opposite bank, standing unseen among the overhanging trees, Shingas looked on. The iron mask of inscrutability slipping from his face at the sight of such innocent pleasure. Reveling in the children's obvious enjoyment, and the sound of Esther's laughter. Basking in the radiance of her smile.

And so, as the weeks passed, the young horse's condition improved. Its muscles and tendons strengthened by the heavy work. Its glossy coat a testament to the healthy diet of corn and hay, and

Esther's healing remedies. But as the horse grew stronger so too did Esther's desire to escape. Impatience welling up inside her like a boil about to burst. Thankfully, she was sensible enough to know that the time had to be right. And that when the chance she hoped for eventually came, it was not wasted. So, trusting in God's good grace she waited patiently for its arrival.

When it came, as she prayed it would, it did so quite unexpectedly. Almost as though a magician had waved his magic wand and shouted "Abracadabra". As usual, Shingas had left his cot just after dawn, Esther watching unseen as he slipped out of their room without a word. Mercifully, since the fateful night in the stream, there had been no further physical contact between them. Keeping to his own bed he had allowed her and the young girl to sleep together. Why that was so she wasn't sure. But it was certainly something she was grateful for. After a simple breakfast, with the young girl at her side, Esther made her way to the coral, and the start of another day scavenging for wood. It was then, as they were leading the horse away that Esther noticed several women with woven baskets standing in a group beside one of the long-houses. Her gaze lingering on them as they moved away into the surrounding forest presumably in search of fruit or berries.

Returning with their first load of firewood, with the horse standing patiently, helped by the young girl Esther began stacking the sticks and branches they had collected onto the depleted woodpile. With the absence of the women, apart from a few warriors lounging about in the shade gossiping, and smoking their pipes, the village appeared strangely empty. In an instant, Esther knew that this was the moment she had been waiting for, and with her heart racing she walked across the longhouse and ducked inside. Reappearing moments later, a laden satchel slung over her shoulder, with a furtive glance towards the group of warriors she made her way back to the wood pile. Lifting the French girl onto the animal's back, taking hold of the lead-rope, she began walking away, willing herself not to hurry. Terrified that at any moment one of the warriors would call after her.

Moving through the crowded trees with the skill of a seasoned hunter the young buck shadowed the group of women. Among them were several young maidens, and one in particular had caught his eye. Edging closer, taking care not to be seen, the young buck looked longingly at the object of his desire. His longing for her growing as she reached out for a handful of berries. The contours of her shapely body accentuated by her tightly fitting dress. Already aware of his presence, turning towards him the young maiden encouraged his attention with a coquettish smile.

Having plundered the bushes of their fruit the group of berry-pickers moved deeper into the forest. Surreptitiously distancing herself from them, the young maiden cast a sly look over her shoulder to see if the young buck was still following. But she needn't have been concerned. Her come-hither smile alone had been enough to seal his fate. With passion burning like a fire in his belly, the young buck continued to shadow her as she moved between the trees supposedly in search of more berries. With the group of women now out of sight, looking back she fixed him with her dark liquid eyes. Smiling a little bolder this time. Sufficiently encouraged, desire coursing through his veins the young buck strode towards her. With her trap sprung, dropping her basket to the ground, not caring that half its contents had spilt out onto the ground, the young maiden slipped away into the trees. Determined not to let her escape, like a wolf chasing down its prey the young buck raced after her. Allowing the space between them to shorten, like a cornered animal, panting for breath she turned to face him. Her firm, young breasts pressed against her doeskin dress, their swollen nipples protruding like little boy's noses.

His throat dry, with passion, the young buck lunged for her. With a quick laugh, spinning on her heels she evaded him with the skill of a matador. Single-minded, arms outstretched he closed on her. Again, she slipped away from him, nimbly eluding his grasping hands. Fueled by frustration in desperation he reached out for her again. Backing away she taunted him with her eyes. She had him now, and with desire welling up inside her, throwing herself onto the ground she pulled up her dress, revealing herself to him. Consumed by lust, the young buck stared down at the prize awaiting him in the silky triangle of black hair. But just as he was about to pull aside his breechcloth the young buck found himself distracted by a sudden movement in the woods ahead of him. Something moving at speed through the crowded trees. Indistinguishable at first but then as it emerged from behind the stand of trees, he could see quite clearly what it was that had distracted him. A look of concern clouding his young face at the sight of the horse with the Yengeese woman Shingas had taken as his wife, and a young child mounted on its back. Unhesitating, with the drumming of the animal's hooves in his ears, all thoughts of the young maiden erased from his mind he began running back towards the village. Behind him, sprawled out on the ground, totally bemused by his actions, the abandoned maiden stared after him, her eyes blazing with anger.

When he reached the village, weaving his way through the cluster of long-house the young buck spotted Tusonderongue, and a group of warriors sprawled out on rush mats outside one of the buildings. Hurrying across to them, stumbling over his words, he told them what he had seen. Concerned by the news, Tusonderongue jumped to his feet, and grabbing the young buck by the arm, he pulled him aside. Was he certain of what he had seen? Could, he be sure? The young buck nodded his head, yes what he had told them was the truth. Satisfied, Tusonderongue turned away and making his way to one of the long houses he slipped inside. Filled with apprehension the young buck waited, doubts creeping into his mind like an unseen enemy. Was he sure what he had seen, or had he acted too hastily? Then he saw Tusonderongue emerging from the long-house with the tall figure of Shingas a step behind, his face like thunder. Approaching the young buck, Shingas' features softened a little.

"You saw them? The Yengeese woman, and the child?" A hint of anger in his voice.

"Yes, on the back of the horse. Running fast." The young buck replied confidently. Any doubts he may have harbored quickly dispelled.

"Which direction did they take?" Shingas asked. Convinced that the youth was telling the truth.

Half turning, the young buck stretched out his arm. Pointing in the direction the runaways had taken. Placing a hand on the young buck's shoulder Shingas squeezed it firmly with his fingers. An expression of gratitude. Then, having learned all he needed to know, turning away, Shingas walked across to his long-house. Slipping inside, he emerged a few moments later musket in hand, his carry-all, and powder horn slung across his shoulder. Stepping forward Tusonderongue looked at him enquiringly. Meeting the warrior's gaze Shingas shook his head. No, he would go alone. He must be the one to bring them back.

Gripping the horse's mane with one hand, her arm raised to protect her from the swishing branches Esther kicked her heels into the horse's flanks, urging the animal on. The drumming of its hooves like a muffled heartbeat as it galloped through the silent forest. Up behind her, her skinny arms wrapped tightly around her waist, the young girl buried her face in Esther's back. Half an hour later, with its neck lathered in sweat, its sides heaving, pulling back on the improvised rein Esther slowed the tired animal to a walk. Thankful for the temporary respite from the jolting ride, the young girl relaxed her vice-like hold. Feeling the tension draining away from the girl's arms, turning her head Esther smiled at her reassuringly. Be brave, all will be well.

Jogging at a pace he could maintain for half a day, following the tracks made by the horse's hooves Shingas slipped through the crowded trees, the heavy musket slung across his shoulder. Although he had been running for two hours, he showed no sign of tiredness. Then he saw them. A sudden glimpse of his quarry moving through the trees ahead of him. Like a runner with the winning line in sight, lengthening his stride, Shingas set off in pursuit. Gaining on them with every stride.

Without knowing why, some sixth sense perhaps, casting a glance over her shoulder the young girl spotted Shingas running through the trees towards them. Terrified by the sudden appearance of the warrior she screamed. The small sound magnified by the enveloping silence of the forest. Turning to see what had frightened the child Esther stared in disbelief at the sight of Shingas sprinting towards them. Stunned at how quickly he had learned of their absence, pushing such concerns from her mind, digging her heels into the horse's side, she kicked the animal into a run. But Shingas caught up with them, matching the horse stride for stride. Reaching out an arm he clutched at the young girl's leg. Shrieking in terror she pulled it away from his grasping fingers. Again, Esther kicked at the horse, driving her heels into its heaving flanks. Her body arched forward over its neck urging it on. Immediately, the horse responded by lengthening its stride. Its powerful legs driving it forward. Its hooves digging into the soft ground as it raced ahead. With the horse at full gallop, stealing a look over her shoulder Esther saw that Shingas was falling behind. Moments later, he was lost from sight altogether.

With day and night colliding, bursting out from the trees Esther pulled on the rein bringing the horse to a halt on a sandy spit beside the edge of a lake. Its tranquil surface shimmering like burnished gold in the rays of the setting sun. Confronted by the vast expanse of water and knowing that Shingas was not far behind them Esther knew that they were trapped. Terrified by the thought of falling into his hands once more, after taking a moment to survey the lake with its palisade of towering trees, she made her decision, they could not go back. With her mind made up, spurring the horse forward Esther urged it on into the deeper water where, much to her relief the young mare instinctively began paddling its front legs. Conscious of the need to lighten the animal's load, freeing herself from the young girl's encircling arms Esther gently lowered herself into the water. Pushing the girl forward with her outstretched arm as she did so. A reassuring smile lighting up the girl's face as she grabbed hold of the horse's mane with both hands. With the child safe on the horse's back, kicking out with her legs Esther began swimming alongside. Extending her arms out in front and drawing them back. Forward and back. Forward and back. Pulling herself through the water. Each stroke taking her further out into the lake. One shoreline fading away behind her. The other beckoning to her like a siren.

As the golden orb of the dying sun began sinking below the western horizon Esther found herself tiring. The stamina needed to drag her arms through the ice-cold water ebbing away. The sodden doeskin dress clinging to her body, weighing her down like a suit of chain-mail. Even keeping her head above the rippling wavelets was a challenge she was slowly losing. In desperation, pulling the strap over her head Esther released her grip on the carry-all. Watching as it slipped from her fingers, disappearing beneath the murky waters of the lake. Taking with it the food she had secretly squirreled away in readiness for their bid for freedom. No longer weighted down by the heavy burden with renewed energy Esther redoubled her effort. But try as she might, inexorably fatigue began taking its toll, and slowly but surely the horse began moving ahead of her.

With her hands knotted in the animal's mane wide-eyed, the young girl stared down at Esther. Her face, a picture of despair as she watched her slipping further behind. Open-mouthed, gasping for air Esther redoubled her effort, and kicking out with her legs she began dragging her tired arms through the water. But as her strength drained away, she soon began floundering, her chin sinking beneath the surface. Horrified, the girl cried out to her. Words Esther couldn't understand but their meanings were clear. Encouraged by the sound of the child's voice, just as the horse started pulling ahead of her in a last despairing effort, reaching out, Esther grabbed its tail. Relief and elation flooding through her as she felt herself being dragged along in its wake.

Standing on the narrow sandy beach Shingas gazed out across the broad expanse of water, a witness to Esther's audacity. Filled with admiration, after losing sight of them in the fading light, turning his back on the lake Shingas moved away into the surrounding trees. The bravery of the Yengeese woman had saved her for now, but Shingas was not about to give up. His pride would not allow it. The humiliation if she were to escape would be too much for him to bear.

Sinking its hooves into the soft gravel, with one final effort the exhausted horse staggered out of the lake, dragging Esther behind it like a landed fish. Safely ashore, sliding down from the animal's back the young girl dashed across to where Esther lay sprawled on the beach, the water lapping at her feet. Falling to her knees she threw her arms around Esther's neck, tears of happiness running down her cheeks. Pushing herself upright, thankful that their ordeal was over Esther hugged the girl to her chest. Overwhelmed by a sense of relief that her gambling had succeeded, and that they were safe, at least for now. While she was under no illusions that what lay ahead of them would not be without its dangers, the fact that they were free was enough for now. Freeing herself from the child's embrace Esther pushed the strands of hair plastered to her face, and climbing unsteadily to her feet, with strength returning to her legs, she walked across to where the horse was standing, completely done in. Wrapping her arms around the mare's broad neck, whispering words of thanks she buried her face into its matted mane. Having expressed her gratitude, running her hand lovingly over the horse's back, taking hold of the rein Esther led the exhausted animal towards the surrounding trees.

With the horse safely tethered to a tree Esther and the young girl began stripping off their wet dresses. Thankful for the warmth of the evening breeze on their naked bodies. After ringing out as much of the water as they could, hanging their clothes from a branch they set about fashioning a bed of sorts from the abundance of fallen leaves. Satisfied with their efforts, trying hard not to think of their supper laying at the bottom of the lake, huddled together for warmth the pair quickly fell into a deep sleep.

As the morning sun climbed into the sky, narrow shafts of sunlight began piercing the canopy of branches. Falling like a spotlight on Esther, and the young Girl asleep together like a pair of spoons on a bed of leaves. Awakened by the touch of sunlight on her skin, sensing something was wrong instinctively, Esther looked across to the surrounding trees. The horse was gone. Taking care not to wake the girl she climbed to her feet, and pulling on her dress, hoping that the horse had gone in search of water, she ran towards the lake.

Emerging from the trees Esther spotted the horse grazing on a narrow grassy margin. With a sigh of relief, conscious that her sudden appearance might spook the animal, she moved cautiously towards it. But no sooner had she taken her first tentative steps when laying back its ears the young mare began backing away from her. Instantly, Esther stopped in her tracks, her heart racing. Terrified that the animal would run off. Waiting for the horse to settle she moved forward again. Her hand held out in front of her as though she were offering it something to eat. Again, the horse raised its head, a front hoof pawing nervously at the ground. Motionless, hardly daring to breathe Esther watched as the horse lowered its head and began grazing on the tufts of yellowing grass. At a loss as to what she should do next, Esther was suddenly distracted by the appearance of the young girl. Watching in horror as she began striding confidently towards the horse, calling out to it in a firm voice, much like a mother chastising a naughty child.

"Mauvais cheval! Mauvais cheval! Toujours vous avez faim. Vous etes un mauvais cheval. Bad horse! Bad horse! Always you are hungry. You are a bad horse."

Pricking up its ears at the sound of her voice, the horse tensed, but rather than galloping off as Esther feared, the animal stood quite still allowing the girl to walk up to it. Running her fingers over the horse's nose by way of a reward, taking hold of the makeshift rein, the young girl led the horse across to where Esther was standing, a look of relief etched on her face.

After a meagre but nourishing breakfast of wild berries, eager to be on her way Esther climbed up onto the horse, and with the young French girl clinging on behind her, taking her directions from the sun she set off. Hampered by the dense woodland their progress was painfully slow, with only the occasional clearing allowing the young horse a chance to lengthen its stride. Thankfully, as the morning wore on the trees became more spaced, the serried ranks of towering firs giving way to stands of ancient hemlocks. Their massive trunks, and sturdy branches worth their weight in gold to any shipbuilder. With the deciduous woodland offering a chance to make better progress, spotting what appeared to be a path, kicking her heels into the horse's flanks, Esther cantered towards it.

Cast into shadow beneath the dense canopy of leaves, peering out through the foliage, Shingas watched with satisfaction as the horse drew nearer. The previous evening, knowing that the Yengeese woman would travel east, taking advantage of the remaining daylight, he had circled the lake. With little hope of finding them in the darkness, using his knowledge of the terrain he decided instead to lay-in-wait close to where a narrow hunting trail, running east to west entered a steep-sided defile. A natural avenue through the wall of trees, especially for anyone on horseback. With the drumming of the horse's hooves growing louder, choosing his moment with a wild yell Shingas leapt out onto the trail. Startled by the man's sudden appearance, whinnying with fear the horse reared up onto its hind legs, throwing off its riders as it did so. Raising his musket Shingas opened fire, the sound reverberating through the woods. With the musket ball lodged in its head, mortally wounded the horse dropped to the ground. Its life snuffed out by an ounce of lead. Horrified by his act of cruelty, clutching the whimpering girl to her, Esther watched as Shingas came striding towards them, his features devoid of emotion. With the two fugitives sprawled at his feet, Shingas stared down at them menacingly. Powerless to defend herself, shielding the girl with her body Esther stared back at him defiantly. If she was to die, she would do so by facing her killer. Slowly the seconds ticked by, and then much to Esther's amazement, having made up his mind, throwing his musket over his shoulder Shingas turned away, and began walking towards the encircling trees. Nonplused, Esther stared after him. Why, having found them, was he now abandoning them? It didn't take long for her to work it out, and with a last fleeting look at the stricken animal, gripping the young girl's hand, she began hurrying after him. With the horse, they had had every chance of escaping. Without it, lost and alone in the forest with no food, save for a few scavenged berries the reality was that their chances of survival were slim indeed. So, resigned to their fate, following in Shingas"s footsteps Esther and the young girl began their journey back to a life of captivity.

It was late evening when Shingas reached the outlying longhouses of the village, and with Esther and the French girl following a few paces behind him, he made his way towards the quadrangle. No sooner had they reached the open space at the heart of the village when people began appearing, men, women and children. All crowding together around its edges, hushed and expectant. Despairingly, Esther scanned the faces of the hostile crowd hoping to catch a glimpse of the old woman. What she saw instead was the figure of the burley woman elbowing her way through the onlookers, the locket Esther had given her in exchange for the child hanging around her neck. Emerging from the crowd she strutted up to Esther, and shouting something unintelligible at her, grabbing hold of the French girl's arm she wrenched her free from Esther's grip. Powerless to intervene shame-faced, Esther watched in dismay as she dragged the struggling girl away. The chorus of approval from the savage audience ringing in her ears.

No sooner had the pair disappeared into the crowd when a hush descended over the onlookers. Perplexed, Esther looked around her, wondering why they had fallen silent. She didn't have long to wait for the answer, as one by one several women began emerging from the crowd, each of them armed with a stout stick or club. Silently forming themselves into two ranks at the center of the quadrangle. One she recognized immediately her beautiful face contorted into a look of pure hatred. It seemed that Meeataho was not going to miss this opportunity to have her revenge. So, this was to be her punishment for running away; recalling the boy's plight on the day she had taken the children down to the stream. Only for her, it would be a gauntlet of angry women and not children who would administer her beating. Frantically, she began searching the sea of faces for a glimpse of Shingas, surely, he would spare her this ordeal? But he was nowhere to be seen. So, with all hope of salvation gone, summoning her last reserves of strength, resigned to her fate Esther began running towards the rows of women. Instantly, a great shout went up, the crowd of people surging forward, each of them clamoring for a better view.

With her right arm raised above her head, Esther entered the aisle between the two rows of women. Each of them eagerly awaiting the opportunity to strike her with their stick or club. Gripped by a steely determination she plunged ahead, blows raining down on her from both sides. Nearing midway, a particularly vicious blow dropped her to her knees but before the woman could strike her again, dragging herself onto her feet Esther staggered on. Each step bringing her closer to the end of her purgatory. Ever-closer to the waiting figure of Meeataho, her club gripped tightly in her hand. Oblivious to the young maiden's presence, as she passed in front of her, thrusting out her leg, she sent Esther sprawling onto the ground. In an instant, Meeataho was standing over her, and with her rival lying helpless at her feet she began beating her mercilessly. Striking at the Yengeese woman as though she were a snake. Her pent-up hatred manifesting itself in every blow she struck. Desperate to protect herself, rolling over onto her back Esther began lashing out with her legs. Frantically trying to fend off the deluge of blows raining down on her. And then suddenly they stopped.

Striding out from the crowd, angered by the unnecessary beating being meted out by the young maiden, grabbing Meeataho by the hair Shingas dragged her away, and snatching the club from her hand he threw her onto the ground. Enraged by his intervention, scrambling to her feet Meeataho glared at him defiantly, her eyes flashing with anger. Raising the club in the air Shingas said something to her, his voice imbued with menace. Shocked by his threats, Meeataho backed away, and with a last hate-filled stare she stormed off into the crowd.

With blood running down her face from the deep cut in her forehead as Meeataho disappeared into the crowd Esther slowly pulled herself onto her knees. Dazed and weakened by her ordeal, suddenly from out of nowhere the old woman was hovering over her, her gnarled fingers gently pushing the matted hair away from Esther's eyes. Expressionless, Shingas stood looking down at them. The Yengeese woman whom he had taken as his wife had received her punishment, now he alone must decide what was to become of her. Whether to take her back as his woman or to disown her for shaming him. Though his pride would never allow him to admit to it he found the choice a simple one to make. For even though she had run away, he knew in his heart that he could not give her up. That he could not allow her to become the wife of another warrior. So, with his decision made, turning towards the old woman he gave an imperceptible nod of the head.

Smiling through blackened teeth the old woman helped Esther to her feet and slipping an arm around her waist she walked her towards their long-house. Reaching the doorway, overcome by a sudden bout of nausea, gripping the doorpost for support, her other hand pressed against her stomach Esther began retching. The old woman looking on knowingly. When the Yengeese woman had run off her world had been plunged into darkness. But now her daughter-in-law had been returned to her, and unless she was mistaken, she was with child.

CHAPTER NINE

Standing beside the cooking-fire Esther slowly stirred the contents of the cooking-pot suspended over it, her other hand resting on her distended stomach. The realization that she was pregnant had struck her hard at first. But from initially being unwanted, as the infant grew within her womb so too did her longing for it to be born. Even before she was sure herself, word of her condition had spread like wildfire among the women. The news thawed their animosity towards her, and everywhere she went she was greeted by smiles, and gestures of kindness. Even the burly woman's frosty heart had thawed a little, allowing the French girl to visit with her from time to time. With her sunburned face, doeskin dress, and moccasins the young girl was now almost indistinguishable from the other children. The transformation enhanced when, after much coaxing, she allowed Esther to plat her hair into a braid.

With the forest buried in snow, and the trees cracking like muskets in the bitter cold, the long winter evenings became a wonderful time for both Esther and the child. Snug in the warmth of the long-house they would gather around the lodge-fires with other families. Laughing, and jesting, the pipe being passed around from hand to hand. Being a part of these convivial gatherings Esther witnessed a gentler, more endearing side to these savage people, and she took enjoyment from it. On special occasions, a wizened old warrior, one of the village's storytellers, the firelight playing on his ancient face would enthrall the gathering with stories of long-dead spirits, and monsters. Striking fear into his superstitious audience with tales of witches and vampires. Although unable to understand what he was saying, Esther and the girl still found themselves as enthralled as the all-believing souls crowded around them feasting on his words.

Even on such joyful occasions Shingas seldom made an appearance, and on the rare times when he did, he would sit apart from them, silent and brooding. Taking no part in the merrymaking. Once Esther had caught him looking at her, his gaze focused on her swollen belly, and even though his features remained unchanged, she had the feeling that he was pleased by her condition. Given the long periods of absence since the night that he had ravished her, she wondered if perhaps it was a feeling of remorse that kept him from sharing her bed. Quickly pushing the thought from her mind. After all, how could someone like her be expected to fathom the depths of such a savage heart? A more likely reason was that he was probably sleeping with Meeataho. Although if this were true, it had made little difference to their relationship, for whenever Esther offered her a friendly smile, the young maiden simply scowled back at her. Despite this lack of engagement on his behalf Esther took great pleasure from these evenings and the sense of belonging they engendered.

It was on one such night that, much to her delight the young girl had turned to her, and pointing a finger at herself had announced that her name was Chantal. Touched by the child's revelation, slowly mouthing the word Esther had responded by telling the young girl her name. Smiling with amusement as the child attempted to repeat it back to her. Although seemingly insignificant, by revealing their identities to one another, it seemed an even stronger bond was formed between them. A sense of unity so strong that it was as though they had been born as sisters. It was then, as she held Chantel in her arms that Esther vowed, regardless of their different nationalities, that she would care for this orphaned waif as though she were her own flesh and blood.

Lifted the spoon to her lips, as Esther sampled the contents of the pot the figure of Chantel suddenly appeared in the doorway.
"Venez vite! Venez vite!. Come quickly! Come quickly!" she called out. Her voice filled with excitement.
Returning the spoon to the cooking pot Esther turned towards her. During the long winter months, they had both tried to learn the language of their captors but finding it too difficult, even for the child's nimble brain, they had quickly given up. Deciding instead to teach each other a few basic words in their own language. And while this was successful to a degree, they quickly fell into the habit of relying on facial expressions, and gestures to converse

with each other. Frustrated by Esther's lack of urgency, Chantal called out again. This time remembering to use the English words Esther had taught her.

"Come quicky! Come quickly!"

Smiling at the girl's impatience, lifting the kettle off the fire, Esther walked towards the doorway.

Engulfed by the bustling throng of people, with Chantal pulling on Esther's arm in the hope that she would walk a little faster, the pair made their way through the village. Reaching the quadrangle, clutching each other's hand they began weaving their way through the gathering crowd until they reached the inner ring of spectators. Unaware of the reason behind this urgent migration Esther was shocked to see Shingas standing in the middle of the open space surrounded by a dozen armed warriors, their faces painted for war. She had not seen him for several days, and as she stared at his face emblazoned with war paint, she instantly recalled the fateful day when she had first seen him. The terrible events that had taken place forever imprinted on her memory. An icy fist closing around her heart as the image of Saul's mutilated body flashed before her eyes.

Sensing that the moment was right Shingas raised his arms in the air, and a hush descended over the watching crowd. Off to one side, huddled together Wapontak and a handful of elders looked on with hooded eyes. Helpless spectators to the events that were about to unfold. Satisfied that he had the people's attention Shingas walked across to a warrior standing a little apart from the others, and seizing a corner of the blanket draped across his shoulders, with a wild shout he pulled it away to expose the latticework of bloody stripes left by the whip. Instantly, gasps of amazement filled the air. Horrified by the sight of the warrior's lacerated back, a great cry went up from the watching crowd. Savoring the moment, thrusting the blanket into the warrior's outstretched hand Shingas turned to face his savage audience.

"Behold my people this is how the English treat the warriors of the Haudenosaunee." He called out, his voice loud and impassioned. His finger pointed towards the warrior who had received the whipping. Pausing for a moment to allow his words to sink in.

"Their redcoat soldiers have defeated our French brothers, and now while their Great Father sleeps, they walk with a broad, and heavy foot upon our land, and treat us like dogs."

Angry murmurs rippled through the crowd. His words striking a chord in many of their hearts.

"These English are not like our French brothers. They do not wish to be our friends, their only desire is to steal our lands away from us, and to drive us into the wilderness." Then in a rising voice. "I say it is time to take up the hatchet and drive these English from our land before we too are swallowed up by them."

With their thirst for blood, and vengeance aroused, the crowd roared their approval. Whipped into a frenzy of hatred the warriors among them surged forward, their war cries resounding into the forest. Pressed in on all sides by the crowd Esther suddenly clutched her stomach, her face contorted with pain. Her contractions had started. A new life was ready to enter the world.

Originally constructed by the French, and standing on high ground overlooking the Venango River, a tributary of the mighty Allegheny River the role of Fort Le Boeuf was to guard the southern end of the portage between French Creek and Lake Eire some fifteen miles upstream. Occupied by the British at the conclusion of the war it was now manned by an Ensign and a garrison of two corporals and eleven privates. Enclosed by a wall of logs driven upright into the ground with loopholes set at intervals from which small arms could be fired, entry to the fort was through a single gate guarded by a square bastion on either side. Perfect vantage points from which to survey the dirt track leading out from the surrounding forest, and the broad reaches of the Venango River below.

Inside the palisaded square a small guardhouse and barracks their plank walls topped by a shingle roof ran the length of one wall. While positioned at the northern end with two of its walls forming a corner of the stockade was a two-story blockhouse. Constructed of logs caulked with mud set on stone foundations, its windowless walls were inset with two rows of loopholes six to each row, forming an impressive defense. Fluttering proudly from its single flagpole was the blood-red cross of St George.

It was one of the corporals who saw them first. Looking to supplement their meagre rations of boiled meat and corn, he had spent his off-duty time down at the river. Returning with a fine catch of bass and perch he stared in disbelief as a large party of Indians, their faces daubed with war paint, emerged from the encircling trees. Cursing the idleness of the sentry on duty, dropping his fishing pole and catch he began sprinting towards the open gates of the fort. Yelling out a warning as he ran.

Hearing the corporals cry, raising his head above the bastion the sentry looked in horror at the horde of Indians raced along the track towards the fort. Instinctively, raising his musket he fired into them. Watching with satisfaction as one of the leading warriors tumbled to the ground. Below him, the corporal had now reached the gates and was frantically trying to push them shut. Without attempting to reload, crossing to the ladder the sentry began clambering down to join him. Inside the fort, alerted by the sound of musket fire clutching their flintlocks, a group of soldiers spilled out from the barracks, their faces etched with concern. Desperately trying to close the gates the corporal called out to them.

"Over here! To the gates, we . . ." The words dying in his throat as with a savage cry a Seneca warrior lashed at him with his hatchet. Its curved blade sliced across the soldier's neck and severing his windpipe.

With Shingas at their head, shrieking their war cries the Seneca warriors began pouring in through the half-closed gate. Engulfed by the onrushing Indians, desperately trying to defend himself the sentry lashed out with the butt of his musket. Evading the soldier's wild swings, pushing the muzzle of his musket into the soldier's chest, Cattawa pulled the trigger. The lead ball tearing through cloth and flesh until it reached his heart. Killing him instantly. Witnessing the death of their comrades and realizing the futility of attempting to close the gates, firing a ragged volley into the Indians the remaining soldiers, seven in number began retreating towards the blockhouse. With several warriors struck by a hail of bullets, shrieking their defiance, the Seneca returned fire. Whooping aloud as three of the soldiers collapsed onto the ground, blood oozing from their wounds. With little hope of reloading their muskets, freeing their bayonets from their belts the four remaining soldiers slowly backed towards the blockhouse, and safety. Ahead of them, knives drawn, a party of Seneca warriors raced towards their three fallen comrades. Fearing the same fate, with bayonets fixed the four men stood shoulder to shoulder. If they were to die, they would take some heathen devils with them. It was then that salvation in the form of the young ensign revealed itself. Appearing in the open doorway of the blockhouse he yelled out to them.

"In here! In here!"

Needing no further encouragement, while their bloodthirsty enemy busied themselves with their scalping knives, the soldiers turned and ran towards the open door. Seeing the beleaguered soldiers fleeing towards the blockhouse, Shingas yelled out a warning. Instantly, a dozen warriors raised their muskets and opened fire. Miraculously, two of the soldiers survived the hail of bullets, and reaching the open doorway they staggered inside. The heavy door slamming shut behind them. Outside the fearful screams of the two less fortunate soldiers were quickly silenced. War clubs and tomahawks doing their bloody work.

With the last of the soldiers now trapped inside the blockhouse Pahotan together with a dozen warriors, all armed with muskets ran towards the soldier's barracks. Once inside they began knocking away some of the planks with the butts of their rifles, giving them a clear view of the blockhouse, and the twin rows of loopholes set at intervals in its walls. Crouching beside the half-open gate, the body of the dead corporal sprawled at his feet Shingas looked across at the blockhouse. Enraged by the futile patter of the musket balls striking its walls, he signaled to a group of warriors armed with bows. Gathering them around him, after passing on his instructions Shingas sent one of them off towards the barracks. As the warrior hurried away, eager to put his plan into action, pulling open the front of the dead soldier's tunic, Shingas went to work with his knife, cutting the coarse material into thin strips.

Once inside the barracks, the warrior quickly found the small storeroom at the far end, and, forcing open the door, he began scouring the crowded shelves. Finding what he had been told to look for, taking down the small keg of oil, he ran out of the building. Delighted by the warrior's find, after shattering its lid with his hatchet, Shingas watched as one by one each warrior dipped an arrow with a strip of the corporal shirt wrapped around its shaft into the oil. With the impregnated cloth set alight, raising their bows they launched their fiery missile into the air. Watching with satisfaction as the blazing arrows rained down on the blockhouse's shingle roof. The flames quickly took hold, their lurid glow illuminating the encroaching darkness.

Square in shape, and no bigger than a large room the interior of the blockhouse offered little in the way of comfort; an iron stove for cooking the meals of those on duty, a table surrounded by a few chairs to eat from, and a pair of lanterns suspended on chains from a rafter. Cut into the walls were rows of loopholes. The lower ones set at the height of a man's shoulder the upper ones reached by a ladder leading up to a narrow gallery landing. Trapped inside the confined space, the four soldiers positioned at the lower loopholes facing into the fort's interior were keeping up a steady fire. The crash of their musket's reverberation off the log walls. Clouds of acrid smoke hanging in the air. Standing side by side at the table, ramrods in hand the young Ensign and a soldier working methodically loading their empty muskets. Thrusting them into the waiting hands of the men at loopholes in exchange for the one they had just fired. The Ensign casting an anxious look up at the burning roof as he worked. Watching the corporal as he carried another bucketful of water up to the gallery in a forlorn effort to extinguish the hungry flames.

Sensing a slackening of the fire from outside, leaning forward one of the soldiers peered out through his loophole. Instantly a hail of musket balls pattered like hailstones against the blockhouse wall. Staggering backwards, a bloody hole where his right eye had once been he slumped to the floor. Staring down at the dead soldier, arming himself with a musket, the loader took his place at the loophole. Behind him, protected from the burning embers falling from the roof by the narrow landing, having given up any hope of putting out the flames, axe in hand the corporal continued hacking away at the loophole in the rear wall. Moments later and another soldier suddenly staggered back from his loophole clutching his face. Cradling the soldier in his arms as the young Ensign lowered the dying man to the floor above them the roof beams finally gave way, sending the blazing roof down on top of them.

Whooping and howling like devils possessed the Seneca warriors watched as consumed by the voracious flames the roof finally caved in. Several of them were showing their bravery by running up to the blockhouse and firing their muskets into it through the lower loopholes. Then without warning, the blockhouse door was flung open, revealing the figure of the young Ensign framed in the doorway, his hair and clothing ablaze. Like a human torch, he staggered out into the stockade his agonizing cries rending the night. Crowding around the pitiable figure, exulting in his agony, the crowd of warriors looked on, watching as his skin began melting like butter. Unable to endure the pain any longer falling to the ground the young Ensign curled his body into the foetus position, surrendering his body to the all-consuming flames.

Outside the stockade, bathed in the lurid glow from the burning building like a nocturnal badger leaving its set, the corporal emerged from the enlarged hole he had managed to make in the blockhouse wall. With nobody alive to join him, setting off at a stumbling run he made his way towards the welcoming darkness of the forest.

Bathed in candlelight, tightening her grip on the two wooden posts driven into the ground on either side of her, Esther cried out as another contraction seized her body. Her whole being urging her to push down. Demanding that she rid herself of the thing which was causing her so much pain. Kneeling at her side the old woman shook her head. Not yet and leaning forward she offered Esther a short stick to bite on. Clenching her teeth Esther turned her head away. Smiling, the old woman climbed to her feet and walking across to the large pot suspended over the fire she removed a piece of doeskin. After ringing out the excess water she returned to Esther and kneeling beside her she began wiping away the beads of perspiration from her daughter-in-law's upturned face.

Another contraction. Stronger this time. And again, the overwhelming urge to push down. Through clenched teeth, Esther stared despairingly at the old woman. Thankful that this time she was nodding her head vigorously, encouraging her to push. With a final scream, consumed by a feeling of exquisite pain Esther felt the baby slipping from her body. Drained, releasing her grip on the two bearing posts she slumped back against the wall. Watching with a slight air of detachment as the old woman scooped the infant up in her arms. Its first lusty cry heralding its arrival into the world, and satisfied that all was well, her wrinkled face creased into a smile she handed Esther her newborn child.

Overwhelmed by a sense of joy, cradling the baby in her arms Esther looked down at her infant's face. From the moment she knew for certain that she was pregnant, she had prayed that she would give birth to a boy. And now here he was. All soft and warm against her skin, his tiny eyes screwed tightly shut, his shock of black hair plastered against his head. She knew that they would give him his name and that he would always be called by it. After all, they were his people. But to her, his name would be Daniel, and when she dared, she would whisper it to him. It had been her brother's name. He had lived four days longer than the woman who had given him life after laboring for two days on the birthing stool. Long enough for him to be baptized. Long enough to be loved and hated in equal measure by the man who had sired him. And, although it did not influence her choice, she also thought it was a fitting name for one who had been born into such a lion's den.

Half-running, half-staggering the corporal moved through the towering trees, eager to distance himself from the fort without losing his way. After spending the night at the edge of a cedar swamp, hardly daring to close his eyes, at dawn he had set out again. Skirting the boggy ground, knowing that his only hope of survival lay in finding the river he moved away into the surrounding trees. With the midday sun high in the sky, after laboring up a steep wooded incline, much to his joy below him he caught sight of a silver horseshoe of water; the Alleghany River. Its gently flowing waters his road to salvation. With his spirits lifted, keeping the river in sight, the pangs of hunger and thirst forgotten he moved on. Later that afternoon away to the north, in the direction of Fort Venango he spotted a plume of black smoke rising above the trees. Evidence that it too had suffered the same fate as Fort Le Boeuf. Filled with despair he plunged back into the forest. The will to survive driving him on.

Sweltering in the heat of the day, cursing their luck and the NCO who had drawn up the duty roster the two sentries, one on each side of the fort's north gate were suddenly alerted by a call from a fellow sentry stationed on the rampart above them. A note of urgency in his voice.

"Look!" He shouted. "There down the road." Pointing with his outstretched arm.

Instantly, the two sentries turned their attention to the dirt road leading to the fort, and the figure of a man staggering towards them. Recognizing him as a fellow soldier, setting aside their muskets they raced towards him. Overcome with relief at the sight of the two soldiers, half dead from hunger, and thirst the exhausted corporal dropped to his knees, muttering his gratitude through parched lips as the two sentries lifted him onto his feet. Reassuring him that all was well, with the NCO supported between them they made their way towards the open gates and safety.

Revived by two fingers of fine French brandy, and the promise of a meal of boiled meat and potatoes to come, escorted by one of the sentries the corporal was led up a flight of stairs, and into a spacious room dominated by a large mahogany desk. Seated at it, letters and books scattered across its faded leather surface was the fort's commander Captain Simeon Ecuyer. A broad-shouldered man with austere features dominated by a strong chin jutting out like the prow of a ship. Held in high regard by all as a professional solder, along with many of his Swiss countrymen he had been commissioned into service with the British army during the war with the French. In his case by no lesser personage than the Duke of Cumberland himself.

Seeing the corporal standing before him on unsteady legs, too weary even to throw up a salute, Captain Ecuyer barked at the sentry.

"Fetch a chair! Quickly now, can you not see the poor fellow is done in?"

Chafing at the officer's words, shouldering his musket, the sentry crossed the room, and lifting one of the heavy wooden chairs positioned on either side of the narrow window he set it down in front of the officer's desk. With a grateful nod to the soldier, the exhausted NCO slumped down, glad to be finally off his feet. With the corporal seated before him, leaning forward across the desk Captain Ecuyer fixed him with a steady gaze.

"Is it true what I am told, that Fort Le Boeuf is destroyed?"

"Aye Sir. Venango too. Both gone." The corporal replied in a steady voice.

Hearing his worst fears confirmed, the officer leaned back in his chair.

"Good God Venango too! Can, you be sure?"

"Sure, as what I have seen with my own two eyes. T"was nothing else could cause such smoke as I saw. And coming from where I knew the fort lay."

"And it was Mingo's who did this? The ones who attacked you?"

"Aye Tis true. Seneca, they were. That much I'm certain of. Came on us without warning they did. A hundred of the murdering devils. Maybe more."

"And there were no other survivors save for yourself?"

"None sir." said the corporal meeting the officer's steady gaze. "Most died a'fore they made the blockhouse. The last ones I seen alive were Ensign Price and young Grey, and they perished in the fire poor souls. I tried to save them lord knows I tried, but the flames were too fierce."

Feeling the man's pain Captain Ecuyer softened his expression.

"Don't reproach yourself. None here doubts your bravery, you have shown as much in bringing us your terrible news." Then turning his head towards the door, he bellowed out. "Orderly! Orderly!"

Immediately, the door was flung open, and a youthful, smartly dressed soldier stepped into the room.

"See to it that this brave fellow is given a hearty meal, and a tot or two of rum to wash it down."

"There are many who say he should be given the whole barrel sir seeing what he's been through." The young soldier replied, a grin spreading across his face.

"Indeed, he does." Ecuyer replied, half smiling at the soldier's impudence. "But I fear a drunken corporal with a head as sore as a Quaker's knee would be a poor reward for their generosity."

Suitably chastised, the orderly quickly crossed the room and helping the corporal to his feet, he escorted him out of the room.

Taking a moment to gather his thoughts, the officer then turned to the sentry standing by the window.

"Find the Sergeant at arms and have him send me an express rider. Oh, and say that he is to saddle my bay gelding."

Sensing the need for urgency, throwing up a hasty salute the sentry hurried from the room. With the room emptied of distractions, eager to transcribe his thoughts into words, dipping his quill into the inkwell, Captain Ecuyer began writing his dispatch.

With less than thirty minutes having passed since the corporal was escorted into the safety of the fort, the gates were flung open once more. The sentries stepping smartly aside as the big bay gelding, its burnished coat gleaming in the bright sunlight passed between them. The horse's hooves kicking up clouds of dust as the express rider spurred it into a gallop.

The road he travelled on had been completed in 1758 during the war with the French. Built with the sweated labor of troops under the command of Brigadier General Forbes whose name it was given. When completed it ran for three hundred miles through the wilderness, from Fort Pitt in the west to the township of Carlisle in the eastern settlements. Although constructed so that troops and supplies could be more easily transported to the isolated outposts along its torturous route. In reality, it was little more than a track hacked through the forest. Snaking its way over hills and gullies, hemmed in for much of its length by towering trees and narrow defiles. But to an express rider, given that it meant three days less in the saddle, the road was as welcoming as a woman's body on a cold winter's night.

After riding for a little over two hours much to his dismay the express rider spotted a column of black smoke rising above the trees not a quarter mile from the road. Torn between his duty, and a desire to offer assistance should it be possible, pricked by his conscience, turning off the road he kicked the horse into a gallop.

Reaching the end of the rutted track, relieved by the sight of the bonfire, the express rider pulled back on the reigns. The pile of burning tree stumps was quite obviously the source of the smoke he had seen and not the work of savages. Swinging around in the saddle he looked across to where a homesteader was straining on a stout pole, the end of it wedged under the roots of an exposed stump. Opposite him, urged on by a freckle-faced boy was an elderly cart horse, harnessed to the tree stump by chains, and a length of rope. Off to the side, an impressive pile of tree stumps bore witness to their labors. Distracted by the sudden appearance of the express rider, shouting something to the boy the man relaxed his hold on the pole. Not happy at having their work interrupted he turned to face the horseman.
"The Indians have taken up the hatchet, best you take your family and go into the fort." The express rider called out, ignoring the man's sullen expression.
No sooner had he finished the sentence when a fair-haired woman in her early twenties, dressed in a simple linen frock, buttoned at the neck and cuffs, came running out from the newly built cabin at the far side of the clearing. Clutching her hand was a young girl no more than five wearing a long gingham dress, her

face framed by ringlets of golden curls hanging halfway to her waist.

"Are we not safe here? We have done them no harm." She called out her face clouded with concern.

Pulling on the reign the express rider turned his horse around until he faced the anxious woman.

"That's as maybe but you must go into the fort. You'll be safe there." Adding with a note of urgency in his voice. "Hurry now the Indians will be here soon."

Behind him, unimpressed by the warning, with a shrug of the shoulders the man turned his attention to the tree stump.

Having delayed long enough, seeing the look of concern on the woman"s face the express rider called out to her again.

"Go to Fort Pitt. Hurry now and all will be well."

Then kicking his heels into his mount, he raced away. The horse's hooves drumming on the sunbaked ground as it broke into a gallop.

Even before the express rider had disappeared from view, filled with trepidation the woman hurried across to her husband.

"Should we not heed his warning?" She asked, fighting to keep the fear from her voice.

Wedging the pole under the half-buried stump the man turned towards her.

"Don"t fret so wife, we're as safe here as in any fort." A condescending tone to his voice.

Unimpressed by his casual assurance she spoke again.

"Should we not do as he says?"

Throwing aside the pole her husband turned on her.

"What abandon our home, and trudge thirty miles on the say so of some express rider." He shouted angrily. "No best we stay here. All will be well, you'll see."

After a grueling two-day ride, stopping only for a few hours at Fort Bedford to rest his tired horse, at dawn the express rider was once more back in the saddle. The urgency of his mission driving him on. Captain Ourry, the fort's commander, had offered him a fresh mount but he had refused. Convinced that there was no better animal to have under him than Captain Ecuyer's Cleveland Bay, plus a desire to finish the task they had been given, together.

With the forest giving way to more open countryside, and fewer trees to shade them from the heat of the July sun, sensing a weariness in the horse's gait, the express rider pulled off the road. Time for a well-earned rest for both of them before the final leg of their journey. Finding a shady spot with a stream nearby, with its thirst quenched, stripping off the horse's saddle, he tethered the animal to a tree. He would dearly have loved to remove his boots, but he knew that if he did, he'd not get them on again, so unbuttoning his jacket instead, after a meagre supper of cold meat and biscuits, with the Bay horse feeding on the last of its oats, with its saddle as a pillow he quickly drifted off to sleep.

Having slept longer than he had intended, with nightfall approaching, stretching some life back into his limbs, the express-rider climbed into the saddle once more, and with a bright moon to guide them, nudging his heels into the horse's sides the express-rider set off along the ever-improving road. Keeping to a steady canter the miles quickly slipped by, and as the first golden rays of sunlight pierced the dawn sky the rider found himself approaching a sentry post on the outskirts of Philadelphia. The broad outlines of its more prominent buildings silhouetted against the lightening sky. Manned by a lone bleary-eyed soldier, reigning in his mount the express rider called out to him.

After a thankless night guarding the good folk of Philadelphia, all safely tucked up in their feather beds, and with the morning chill creeping into his bones, the sentry was not in the best of moods. Even the prospect of tucking into a hearty breakfast in little over an hour seemed to have little effect on his grumpy disposition. And now to make things worse, he had to deal with the demands of this damn horseman. Stepping out from the improvised shelter which served as a sentry box the soldier positioned himself in the center of the narrow road.

"Who goes there? State your business." He called out", his tone of voice as unfriendly as his demeanor.

Resting the reins on the horse's neck, fighting back his impatience, the express rider called out to him again.

"I have an urgent dispatch, and I need directions to the 60th Regiment of Foot."

Chaffing at the bluntness of the man's request, already blessed with an infantryman's inherent dislike for anyone on horseback, especially a fellow soldier, determined to make him pay for his rudeness, holding his musket at the ready the sentry replied.

"And whom might this dispatch be from then?"

Unable to restrain his anger the express rider shouted back at him.

"What I carry and who it is for are no concern of yours. Now point me in the direction of the 60th Regiment of Foot or so help me I'll ride you down and find them myself."

Stung by the rider's words yet determined to prolong the confrontation; the sentry shouted back at him.

"That may be so, but you'll see nothing of the 60th till I'm told..."

But before he could complete the sentence the express rider spurred his horse forward.

"Damn your questions, I'll have those directions or so help me I'll ride you down and find the 60th for myself." His voice filled with venom.

"There's no need for threats", the sentry replied, taking a step back. "I have a duty you know."

"Bugger your duty", shouted the express rider. "I'll have those directions, or the Colonel himself will hear of this, and I doubt he'll treat you kindly for delaying his dispatch." Adding by way of a threat. "More likely a few licks of the cat across your back."

Realizing that he had gone too far, raising an arm the sentry pointed towards the town.

"Follow the road for a mile, and where it forks take the road to the left. Tis no more than a track but it will take you to the 60th."

Without bothering to reply, digging his heels into the horse's flanks the express rider spurred the horse forward. An amused smile transforming his face as the sentry flung himself out of the horse's path. Settling in his saddle, with the sound of the sentry's curses ringing in his ear, the express rider urged the horse into a gallop. The distant rooftops ahead of them as welcoming as a sweetheart's open arms.

Set in five acres of parkland, and approached by a wide sweeping driveway lined by an avenue of towering beech trees Colonel Bouquet had chosen a fine imposing Georgian mansion for his headquarters. Fronting the grand house was a large rectangular lawn with a tall flagpole at its center. The flag of St George fluttering in the warm breeze. With their ceremonial duty completed, the two ranks of redcoats marched back along the road. Their bayonets gleaming in the early sunlight, highly polished boots crunching on the road's graveled surface. Striding along beside them, the chest pushed out, his chin tucked in, spotting the express rider galloping towards them, their sergeant bellowing out a command. Immediate, in perfect time without breaking stride the two files parted like the Red Sea allowing the express rider to gallop between them. The soldier's not best pleased by the clouds of dust settling on their scarlet coats as they returned to their previous formation.

Reigning in his tired mount in front of the house, easing himself down from the saddle, the express rider made his way towards its imposing entrance. Guarded by a pair of sentries, without bothering to issue a challenge, seizing hold of its gleaming brass handle, one of them quickly pushed open the door. It seemed the sight of the mail pouch slung across his chest was all that was required for him to gain access. No sooner had the express rider entered the cavernous hallway when he was confronted by a fearsome-looking Sergeant at Arms. His duty sash worn like a bandoleer over his scarlet jacket. The NCO"s stern expression softened a little at the lines of fatigue etched into the express rider's face.
"Well lad, so you have some news for us, do you?"
"Aye, Sergeant. I . . . I have an urgent dispatch from Fort Pitt." said the express rider, stumbling over the words.
"Follow me, lad." And striding purposefully across the polished, marbled flagstones, he crossed to a pair of ornate double doors. Pulling them open, with a wave of his arm the NCO ushered the

express rider inside, closing the doors behind him with barely a sound.

Although not overly large, as with most Georgian houses, the room was well-proportioned. Its high ceiling embellished with ornate cornices, and molded plasterwork in the form of cherubs, and frothy clouds. Devoid of color, the walls were brightened by a number of framed oil paintings. Some depicting Constable-like landscapes. With others more military in their style and composition. Positioned beneath a large ornate mirror was the room's only item of furniture; an impressive bow-fronted mahogany sideboard, its highly polished surface festooned with fine silver plate, and cut-glass decanters. Occupying the square of richly embroidered carpet which covered much of the boarded floor were a group of English officers resplendent in their scarlet uniforms. The twin rows of gold buttons which embellished their tightly fitting jackets gleaming in the early-morning sunlight allowed in through the tall sash windows. One or two of them glancing impatiently into the adjoining room, which in contrast to the relative calm of the salon was a hive of activity. Serving as the main dining room, uniformed orderlies were already busy setting the long central table, with others arriving carrying domed-topped salvers filled with all manner of breakfast fare. The mouth-watering aroma of fried bacon tainting the air.

Alerted by the opening and closing of the doors, becoming aware of the express-rider's presence, the officer's conversations gradually subsided into a hushed silence. Standing nearest to the doors a youthful-looking lieutenant with a pallid face turned towards him.

"Well, man don't just stand there. State your business." His voice betraying his annoyance at the prospect of having his breakfast delayed.

Prompted by the officer's demand, opening his mail pouch the express rider removed a folded document.

"If you please, Sir", said the express rider. "I have an urgent dispatch for Colonel Bouquet." Holding out the folded document as he spoke.

Instantly, from the far side of the room, a shout went up. A single excited cry, and with a path opening before him Colonel Bouquet emerged from the covey of officers. Of medium height and built with a rotund stomach straining energetically at the buttons of his waistcoat, there was little that was remarkable about him. Blessed with a full head of dark hair, a long slender nose, and a well-proportioned chin, without the presence of a uniform he might easily have been taken for a scholar. The twinkle in his dark eyes, a clue to a lighter side to his nature. When he spoke, his voice betrayed a slight European accent. A testimony to his Swiss lineage.

"Ah! News at last." He cried, a bright smile illuminating his face as he took the dispatch from the express rider's outstretched hand. "Where have you come from lad?"

"From Fort Pitt sir."

"A goodly ride then? For which you have our grateful thanks", said Bouquet before turning to one of his officers.

"Captain Basset please be so kind as to instruct the duty Sergeant to take this brave fellow to the kitchen. Tell him he is to be given a hearty breakfast, and although tis early in the day, perhaps a toddy or two to wash it down. But no more than that." Adding wistfully as he looked into the express rider's tired, face. "For sadly I fear I may have need of his services before the day is out."

Nodding his head in acknowledgement, the express rider turned away and following on the heels of the officer he left the room. Behind them, filled with a sense of trepidation, breaking the wax seal Colonel Bouquet unfolded the dispatch. The group of officers were crowding around him expectantly.

Within the hour, after feasting on rashers of bacon as thick as his finger, and more eggs than he'd eaten in a month all washed down with a generous tot of rum, furnished with a fresh mount the express rider climbed into the saddle. In his mail pouch was a copy of Captain Ecyer's letter together with a dispatch from Colonel Bouquet himself. A hurriedly written document, but one which wholeheartedly supported Captain Ecyer's concerns. A letter expressing in the gravest of terms the need for urgent and immediate action by his Commander-in-chief. A fervent request that Fort Pitt and the surrounding area be given protection against the marauding savages whose war parties were even now roaming the western frontier of Pennsylvania. Attacking isolated settlements, and laying waste their inhabitants" homes, and fields. And so aware of their importance, and the trust placed in him to see them safely delivered, spurring his horse into motion the express rider began his journey to New York, and the residence of the Governor-General himself.

Alone in his library with its heavily laden bookshelves lining all but one of its four walls. The latter accommodating three full-length casement windows, their heavy, brocaded curtains drawn against the sunlight. Pausing to adjust his steel-rimmed spectacles, Sir Jeffrey Amhurst continued reading the letter delivered to him less than an hour ago. His aristocratic features, marred somewhat by a wide down-turned mouth mirroring the feeling of outrage welling up inside him as he continued reading its contents. In his late forties, dressed in a dark suit, which although plain in style was exquisitely tailored, and a white shirt ruffled at the neck, and wrist, his clothing alone was ample proof of his exalted position. The dispatch from Fort Pitt with news of the loss of Fort Le Boeuf and Fort Venango, while pricking his conscience for having persistently flattered himself that the uprising was an alarm that would soon subside. It also brought forth a determination in him to stamp out this infamy, and to punish those villains responsible. So, with his thoughts in order, crossing to the impressive walnut desk which dominated the room, seating himself in the leather-bound captain's chair, quill in hand he began writing his reply to Colonel Bouquet's dispatch.

Sir, Today I received your dispatch with news of the loss of our posts at Venango and Le Boeuf and I intend to take every measure in my power to severely chastise those infamous villains who carried out this vile crime against His Majesties subjects. To this end, I have issued orders for Major Campbell to join you immediately with the light infantry companies of the seventeenth, forty-second and seventy-seventh Regiments. Thus, reinforced you are to proceed with all speed to Fort Pitt and secure the garrison against the savages. Should any Indian tribes take up arms against you they are to be met with such force that is necessary to reduce them to reason. No punishment we can inflict is adequate to the vile crimes of these inhuman villains and I only need add that I do not wish to hear of any prisoners being taken. My orders are that should any savages who dare to take up arms against you, fall within your power that they are to be put to death. Yours Sir Jeffery Amherst, Commander-in-Chief.

CHAPTER TEN

With the end of July approaching, after a delay of some eighteen days while wagons, and draught animals, plus provisions for the campaign were assembled, Colonel Bouquet and his little army of five hundred men finally broke camp and began their march. Riding at the head of the column with his officers, looking back over his shoulder Colonel Bouquet surveyed his little force as it tramped along the street behind him. The sight of sixty invalid soldiers, each too weak to march, being transported in open wagons doing little to bolster their confidence in their enterprise. And while unafraid of what might lie ahead, it was nevertheless a sobering reminder of the inadequacy of the force under his command to carry out the ambitious and dangerous task entrusted to them. A reminder also of the hundreds of soldiers who had lost their lives over the last seven years in the wilderness which lay ahead of them. A thought which was never far from his mind.

Clear of the town, marching three abreast, the bare-legged Highlanders of the 42nd regiment. The Black Watch in their kilts and plaids and the Grenadiers in their scarlet coats began winding their way along the Cumberland valley. The sight of the isolated cabins deserted or burnt to the ground, that they passed a chilling reminder of the dangers which lay ahead of them. Following behind the ranks of soldiers, lumbering over the bumpy track was the convoy of heavy wagons, each drawn by a team of oxen and flanked by a guard of Light Infantry. Bringing up the rear were some two hundred packhorses heavily laden with supplies and sacks of flour. Each string of a dozen horses held in check by a pair of drivers hired for the task at Colonel Bouquet's insistence.

On the fourth day after a grueling trek along the badly neglected pioneer road, Colonel Bouquet's little army marched into the frontier settlement of Bedford. The heartening sound of the Grenadiers March played on fife and drum music to the ears of its inhabitants. Hemmed in by the encircling mountains, the village boasted a dozen or so log cabins each surrounded by a strip of cultivated ground and the beginnings of an apple orchard. Dominating the small settlement was an impressive fort, named along with the scattering of dwellings clustered around it after no lesser peerage than the Duke of Bedford himself. Standing on raised ground above the west bank of the Juniata River, the fort's star-shaped construction boasted a bastion at each of its five points with a deep ditch, and a rampart of earth thrown up around it. Lacking a well, to secure a ready supply of water from the river a wooden causeway with a planked roof had been constructed, offering a degree of protection for the water carriers should they come under attack.

Alerted by the music, families began leaving their cabins. Each one of them filled with astonishment, and joy at the sight of so many soldiers tramping down the dusty road towards them. Unable to contain their relief, pushing open the fort's southern gate hundreds of wretched fugitives who had fled their homes, and sought sanctuary in the fort, spilt out. Their clamorous shouts drowning out the music. While from the ramparts above, their rousing cheers adding to the din the meagre garrison looked down on the approaching column with glad hearts.

With the joyful cries of his men ringing in his ears, striding out through the gates Captain Lewis Ourry the fort's commanding officer, his portly figure threatening the constraints of a uniform at least one size too small, approached the group of mounted officers. Throwing up his hand in a semblance of a salute as he did so. Returning the officer's salute, climbing down from his horse, with a smile lighting up his face Colonel Bouquet accepted the officer's outstretched hand. The pair were old friends, having been commissioned into the Royal American Regiment in 1756. Bouquet as the commanding officer of the first battalion with Ourry as his quartermaster.
"As always sir your appearance is both timely and welcomed." said Ourry, trying hard not to affect his voice with too much gratitude without diminishing the warmth of his welcome.
"And I, Sir", replied Bouquet with a contrived grimace, "have had enough of the saddle for one day."

Suitable ensconced in Captain Ourry's quarters above the south bastion, Colonel Bouquet stepped back from the basin of hot water, and taking the towel offered to him he began drying his face. Relieved of the towel Ourry walked across to a long oak table, and picking up a crystal glass decanter he began filling a pair of matching glasses with generous amounts of port. Exchanging the towel for the glass, with a nodded thanks Colonel Bouquet strode over to the window overlooking the parade ground. Peering out, it seemed that every inch of open space within the fort was occupied by a makeshift shelter housing a displaced family or his oxen and wagons. All glad to be safely confined within its stout walls. Satisfied, he turned away, and raising the glass to his mouth he took a long swallow, savoring the warmth of the dark-red wine on his parched throat. A question lingering on his lips.

"So, Lewis what news of Fort Pitt?"

In response to the question, pulling open a desk drawer Ourry removed a folded sheet of paper.

I received this letter from Captain Ecuyer three weeks ago. There has been no word since." said Ourry, placing the letter in Bouquet"s outstretched hand.

Returning his half-empty glass to the table, taking full advantage of the light from the window, Bouquet began reading its contents.

Fort Pitt July 16th
Sir, we have alarms from and skirmishes with the Indians every day; but they have done us little harm as yet. Yesterday I was out with a party of men when we were fired upon and one of the sergeants was killed, but we beat off the Indians and brought the man in with his scalp on. Last night the bullock guard was fired upon when one of the cows was killed. We are obliged to be on duty night and day. The surrounding woods are full of prowling Indians whose number seems daily to increase; but we have plenty of provisions and the fort is in such a good posture of defense that with God's assistance, we can defend it against a thousand Indians. Yours Respectfully et cetera. Simeon Ecuyer.

"Three weeks ago, you say." said Bouquet, carefully folding the letter.

Ourry nodded his head but said nothing.

"I pray we are in time." said Bouquet, retrieving his glass. The words spoken more in hope than certainty.

Before Ourry could reply there was a sudden knock at the door, followed immediately by the appearance of a man's head topped by a black, felt tricorne hat.

"Beg pardon sir but the gentlemen you were expecting are here."

"Show them in lad", said Ourry, swigging down the last of his port.

"Aye sir", replied the soldier, pushing open the door, and calling out in a robust voice. "The captain will see you now."

In response to the soldier's invitation the three men, all of middle age, and wearing a coarse woolen jacket and buckskin breeches walked into the room. Their faces devoid of emotion with a cursory nod towards Ourry they turned towards Colonel Bouquet. Two of them demonstrate their displeasure at being summoned to the meeting by folding their arms across their chest.

"Thank you for coming Gentlemen", said Bouquet, undeterred by the pair's hostile posturing "I will speak frankly, I am ordered by my Commanding Officer to proceed with all haste to Fort Pitt and to secure it against the Indians. To do so I intend to leave behind a greater part of my oxen and wagons and to take only such supplies as I can on packhorses, which hopefully you can supply me with. Also given that my troops are no woodsmen, knowing the wild nature of the country, and the opportunities it presents for ambush, I am also seeking to procure from amongst you as many woodsmen as possible to march with us."

Taking a moment to digest what was being asked of them, after exchanging glances, the spokesman for the group stepped forward, and while his reply was not a refusal, his words offered little in the way of hope.

"Tis our understanding Colonel that most men would prefer to remain here for the defense of their home, and their families."

"I can well understand their concerns", Bouquet replied, knowing full well that there would be some measure of resistance to his requests. "And for my part, to relieve them of such concerns I would be willing to leave additional troops at the fort for the protection of their families."

"Aye know doubt the ones so full of fight that you must transport them in wagons." said one of the other men sneeringly. Mockery dripping from every word. "What use are they to us pray tell me?"

Don't judge these men too harshly or too readily sir", Bouquet replied, fighting back his anger at the man's unfounded assertion. Determined that his words alone, and not how he said them would be enough to rebuke the man's insolence. "These brave fellows are no malingerers but are merely weakened by fever. A malaise contracted while fighting the King's enemies in Havana, and I for one would happily entrust my own family's welfare to them. Safe in the knowledge that I should not find them wanting."

With his sneer replaced by a scowl, dropping his head the man turned, and walked towards the door quickly followed by his two companions. Last to leave, before stepping outside the spokesman turned towards Bouquet.

"You shall have your horse's Colonel. I cannot say either way on the other matter except that I will speak in favor of it to any that will consider accompanying you."

"I thank you, sir. I shall march for Fort Pitt in two days from now."

With a curt nod, the man left the room, closing the door behind him.

"Damn their insolence." Ourry blurted out, angered by the settler's unwillingness to offer more assistance.

Smiling at Ourry's outburst, Bouquet crossed to the table and picked up the decanter. He proceeded to fill both glasses to the brim with what remained of the port. Taking care not to spill a drop, with a smile playing at the corner of his mouth, he handed one of the glasses to Captain Ourry.

"Don't think too harsh of them Lewis. I knew well enough that given their miserable suffering, and with Indian war parties raiding all along the border, butchering men, women and children what I asked of them would be hard to countenance.

Knowing better than to pursue the subject further, after downing half the contents of the glass in a single swallow, Ourry quickly changed tack.

"So, Colonel I'm to be reinforced with your idle reprobates, am I?" said Ourry gazing out through the window at the hive of activity in the quadrangle below.

"Indeed, you are sir, all sixty of them." Bouquet replied, with a feigned look of disapproval. His amused tone of voice speaking volumes for the friendship between them.

"And for this, I am no doubt to express my gratitude?"

"Come Lewis a day or two of fresh air, and a more suitable diet will see their health improve beyond measure."

"You forget, Sir", Ourry replied with a knowing look, "that I am privy to the course nature of these fellows and am well aware of the opportunities for debauchery afforded them in Manilla for the price of the King's shilling. So, I doubt fresh air and superior victuals alone will prove a cure for the disease that afflicts them."

That my good sir", replied Bouquet, feigning a sense of indignation, "is a subject on which you must speak about with someone more medically knowledgeable than I." Concluding in a more serious voice. "In truth, I wished I could spare you more able-bodied men, but I fear I shall need all the troops at my disposal if I am to succeed in my task."

"Forgive my levity, sir, I am indeed grateful for the additional troops, and I only mock their condition out of sympathy for it." Said Ourry, a little more contritely.

"Nonsense", said Bouquet, draining the contents of his glass. "I'm sure you mean them no ill will." But enough of this chattering", glancing towards Ourry's desk as he spoke. "For I have a dispatch to write, and an express to get on his way while there is still light enough for him to ride by."

Two hundred miles to the west, seated on her low cot the contented infant cradled in her arms, Esther looked across at the old woman. Her hands busy with an awl, and a length of catgut putting the finishing touches to a cradle-board for her new grandson. Distracted by a movement in the corner of her eye she turned to see the imposing figure of Shingas framed in the doorway. His savage features still emblazoned with war paint. The bloody scalp of the hapless corporal hanging from his belt. Taking in the scene of domesticity, setting aside his musket Shingas walked across to Esther, his gaze focused on the baby she was holding in her arms.

"You have a fine son", said the old grandmother, looking up from her work.

Unmoved by her words, his features as always devoid of emotion, Shingas remained silent, his eyes fixed on the infant. Gripped by a feeling of apprehension Esther looked up at him. Becoming a little afraid.

"Give me the child", demanded Shingas, holding out his arms.

Instinctively, Esther pulled away, clutching the infant to her chest. Although she hadn't understood what he had said, his actions were plain enough.

"Give me the child", said Shingas, the same hard tone in his voice. Plainly it was not a request.

Despairingly, Esther turned and looked at the old woman seated across from her. Meeting Esther's imploring stare the old woman slowly nodded her head.

Comforted a little by the woman's reassurance, holding out her arms reluctantly Esther handed him his son.

With the infant safely cradled in his arms Shingas made his way out from the village, and into the surrounding forest. For more than an hour he walked through the labyrinth of towering trees, the forest floor climbing away before him. Each slope leading to another even higher one. Their craggy sides littered with rocks and the skeletons of fallen trees. Eventually, with shafts of sunlight piercing the thinning canopy like bolts of celestial light, his heart-pounding Shingas reached the final peak. Its naked summit crowned by an outcrop of weathered boulders each one as old as Christendom itself. At their highest point jutting out like a cantilevered balcony was a single giant slab of granite. A promontory so precariously balanced it seemed that it only needed a butterfly to settle on its tip to send it toppling into the void below.

With the wind swirling about him, stepping onto the rock, its surface as flat as a table-top, stretching out his arms Shingas raised the naked infant above his head, and standing like a figure cast in bronze he gazed out at the unbroken panorama before him. An unending wilderness of forest-covered mountains, and valleys encrusted with lakes and serpentine rivers stretching for as far as the eye could see. The world as God had created it. The lands of the Seneca.

With the evening shadows lengthening, and the baby none the worst for its lengthy outing Shingas returned to the long-house. Entering the family's compartment, finding Esther stretched out on a bed of furs seemingly asleep with the infant cradled in the crook of his arm Shingas settled himself on the cot opposite. Lost in devotion he gazed down at his infant son, the child's tiny hands taking an interest in the bear-claw necklace around his neck. Unnoticed, peering through half-open eyes Esther watched in disbelief at the tenderness of the scene. Hardly daring to believe what she was witnessing. That this savage who she feared and hated could be capable of such affection was almost beyond comprehension. Moments later a warrior suddenly appeared in the doorway, and the spell was broken. Climbing to his feet, Shingas snatched up his musket and carefully covering the baby with a blanket of fur he slipped away. Confident that he would not be returning, leaving her cot Esther picked up the infant, and pulling down the front of her dress she held him to her swollen breast.

CHAPTER ELEVEN

On the 28th of July, after resting for a further day while additional supplies of flour were sent out from Carlisle fifty miles to the east, Colonel Bouquet's army of no more than five hundred men was, at last, ready to depart. And with a bright morning sun already warming the air, accompanied by the insistent rattle of a kettledrum the Grenadiers and Highlanders broke camp, and began forming up in their ranks.

At the center of the convoy, flanked on both sides by a company of Light Infantry the heavy wagons, each drawn by a team of oxen were brought into line. Behind them, mooing in protest were a small herd of cattle held in check by a half-dozen stick-wielding drovers. At the rear of the lengthy convoy, roped together in strings of a dozen or so, each managed by a driver, were the packhorses. The clouds of dust thrown up by their hooves clogging the nostrils of the rear-guard of Grenadiers and settling on their blood-red jackets.

At the head of the column Colonel Bouquet and his officers, fortified by a breakfast of cold ham, and freshly boiled eggs washed down by cups of steaming coffee, watched proceedings with a critical eye. Also looking on were a group of thirty or so backwoodsmen. Dressed in their usual fringed hunting frocks, with chins resting on the barrel of their muskets, they viewed the scene of orderly chaos with an air of bored indifference. Among them, with more reason than most for joining what appeared to some to be a foolhardy enterprise were Samuel and Adam Endicote. After a year of brooding inactivity, the older man had seized on the opportunity when it presented itself. More than happy to use any pretext to satisfy his desire for revenge.

Having been advised by the company sergeants that all was ready, throwing a farewell salute to Captain Ourry looking down from the fort's ramparts like a king in his castle, kicking his horse into a walk Colonel Bouquet led his army out of the small settlement. Lining both sides of the street, crowds of displaced settlers looked on in silence as the column tramped its way towards the surrounding wilderness. Straining their necks for a last glimpse of a scarlet jacket before the little army disappeared beneath the verdant arches of the forest. Surrounded by an impervious wall of trees, with a party of backwoodsmen ahead of them as a deterrent against a surprise attack, the convoy of troops, and wagons trudged along what remained of the Forbes Road. In among the party of backwoodsmen following along behind the company of Grenadiers guarding the train of packhorses, with every step Samuels" hopes for revenge grew stronger. The desire for retribution fanned by the wind of hatred.

On the fifth day, they reached the main ridge of the Alleghany Mountains and began the long, torturous climb towards its peak. Slogging up its densely wooded heights. Zigzagging around rocky outcrops, and the decaying trunks of fallen trees. The oxen panting as they pulled the heavy wagons over the rugged terrain. Each soldier cursing the thickness of his uniform as they sweated in the July heat. After two days at long last, they reached the summit. Gazing in awe at the unending wilderness of forest-covered mountains stretching before them. A sea of green which seemed to go on forever, dappled by the shadows of passing clouds rolling over them like wind-blown galleons.

Thankfully, after descending the ridge the country became less rugged. The trees were less dense, and without rocks, and half-buried stumps to impede the wagons they made good time. On the sixth day, after stopping to rest and water the stock at a small stream, to everyone's great joy they arrived at the little outpost of Fort Ligonier.

Standing on a low hill beside the Loyalhanna Creek some fifty miles from Fort Bedford, the fort's principal purpose was to protect the passage of supplies onwards to Fort Pitt positioned at the confluence of the Alleghany and the Monongahela rivers. Constructed in 1758, although smaller in size than Fort Bedford, with its high walls set in a square, and a roofed bastion at each corner, its appearance was as equally as impressive. Lying just outside, encircled by a deep ditch were a cluster of sturdy outbuildings comprising of a sawmill, a smokehouse and a forge. Entry to the fort was through a central gateway defended by a wooden palisade. Its spacious interior boasting an officer's mess, a guardhouse, a quartermaster's store and a large barracks. Glad though they were to set eyes on its ramparts, what pleased Bouquet's weary troops more was the sight of the cross of St George fluttering from its flagpole.

Waiting at the gates, as welcome to see such a large body of troops as they were to have reached the safety of the outpost, was the fort's commander Lieutenant Archibald Blane. A doughy Scot, and an officer not unknown to Colonel Bouquet having previously angered the colonel by proposing that the fort should be abandoned. Thankfully, since then with his request stringently denied, by resolutely defending the post against marauding Indians with only a garrison of seven soldiers, he had restored the Colonel's faith in his integrity, thus ensuring a cordial meeting between the two. After exchanging a customary salute, climbing down from his horse Bouquet shook the officer's outstretched hand. Enquiring as he did so.

"Did the reinforcements I dispatched arrive?"

"Indeed, they did Colonel, and never was I so glad to see a tartan kilt or to welcome such fine soldiers."

"Then all is well?"

"Aye Colonel all is well. Since my last dispatch, we have only been attacked on two further occasions. The second, on the twenty-first being the most serious when they fired on us for the better part of the day."

"Casualties?" Asked Bouquet.

"None, Sir.", said Blane, a little surprised by the brusqueness of the question. "It would appear that good fortune has not deserted us."

"Excellent! Excellent! And what news of Fort Pitt?"

"Sadly, there is little to tell, Sir, for I have heard nothing from them since the thirtieth of May, and though two expresses have gone through from Bedford not one has returned."

Although disturbed by this news, keeping his disappointment to himself, Bouquet's thoughts turned to the safety of his men and supplies.

"Have you room in the fort for my wagons and horses?"

"Indeed, Colonel, and also space in the barracks for some of your men should you want. I am certain they would welcome the comfort of a cot after so many nights spent on the hard ground."

"Thank you but no. The men are quite used to their tents, and weary as they are, the hard ground will not cause them to lose sleep. But if you've no objections, I and my officers will accommodate ourselves in your officer's quarters." The words conveying an intention rather than a request.

With matters settled between them, after receiving reports from his officers that his wishes for the safety and welfare of his force had been carried out Colonel Bouquet retired to his allotted quarters. With much to occupy his mind, although wearier than he would care to admit, the real reason being to find some solitude rather than an opportunity to rest. For though Fort Pitt was less than three days' march away, given the perilous route which lay ahead, with the very real possibility of an ambush, there was much for him to think about.

An hour or so later having cleared his mind of the thoughts which had concerned him, and with his plans for the following days in order, keen to stretch his legs before supper Colonel Bouquet left his quarters. Making his way passed the teams of oxen and horses corralled behind the heavy wagons, some already asleep on their feet he climbed the ladder up to the walkway running along the inside of the wall. Nodding an acknowledgement to the sentry on duty, hands clasped behind his back he began strolling along the narrow platform. Reaching midway, he stopped and gazed down on the neat rows of tents below, the soldier's muskets propped up beside them like sheaves of corn. The murmur of men's voices carrying up to him on the warm night air. It seemed that no matter how weary they were after a grueling day's march, there were still some who found the energy for conversation. Smiling, he turned away, his heart filled with admiration at the uncomplaining nature of his men. Praying that with God's good grace, they would all be delivered safely to Fort Pitt.

Returning to the officer's quarters, seduced by the tempting aroma of roasting meat wafting out from the kitchen, Colonel Bouquet made his way to the mess-room. Illuminated by a pair of matching candelabra the long table which ran down the center of the room was already laid with pewter plates and forks. The half-a-dozen or so off-duty officers seated around it quickly jumping to their feet when he entered the room. Acknowledging their deference with a nod of the head, making his way to the head of the table Colonel Bouquet seated himself in the vacant chair. Moments later, accompanied by the sound of chairs scraping against the wooden floor as the officers returned to their seats, two orderlies entered the room. One carrying a large wooden board topped with an impressive joint of roast beef. The other holding a tureen piled high with freshly boiled potatoes. Setting them down on the table, quietly hoping that there would be enough meat left for their own supper, the two men then left the room. Even before the door had closed, jumping to his feet the young Lieutenant from the Seventy Seventh regiment quickly snatched up the two-pronged fork and carving knife strategically placed on either side of the joint.

"With your permission sir?" He asked, looking towards his commanding officer.

Smiling at the young officer's undisguised enthusiasm, Bouquet waved his hand permissively, watching with undisguised amusement as the young officer attacked the joint with unrestrained enthusiasm. Spurred on by his fellow officers, the clatter of pewter plates striking the table as each of them demanded to be given the first slice.

With the meal concluded and all three bottles of fine claret, seconded with Lieutenant Blane's blessing from the quartermaster's store drained of their contents, banging the bone handle of his fork down hard on the table Bouquet brought the room to order.

"Gentlemen your attention." Pausing to allow their conversations to subside. "Before approaching the business at hand, I would like to extend my sincere thanks to Lieutenant Blane for providing us with such an excellent supper." His sentiments were greeted by shouts of "Here! Here!" from his fellow officers. "Now to the business at hand." said Bouquet, continuing once silence had been restored. "Given that no news has been received from Fort Pitt for many weeks, and with little intelligence concerning the whereabouts of the enemy, I have resolved to press on with all haste. To do so I intend to leave behind the oxen and wagons, and to carry such supplies as we may need including all the flour, on packhorses." His words are greeted by a unanimous nodding of heads from the assembled officers. "Furthermore, given that our route will take us through the treacherous pass at Turtle Creek, and fully aware of the opportunity it offers for ambush, I propose that we process only as far as Bushy Run station. Here we will rest until nightfall, and then by a forced march, under cover of darkness undertake the crossing of Turtle Creek. Are there any questions?"

"What of my reinforcements Colonel, am I to keep them?" Enquired Lieutenant Blane, climbing to his feet. Concerned that there had been no mention of them.

"That you shall Lieutenant but since I cannot risk reducing my force, from necessity they will be fewer in number, and made up of those who are judged too infirm to endure the march ahead."

Feeling somewhat hard done by but knowing that there was little point in objecting, Lieutenant Blane returned to his chair.

Casting a look around the table and seeing that there were to be no more questions, placing his hands on the table for leverage Bouquet pushed himself up from his chair. The other officers quickly clambered to their feet as he did so.

"It has been a tiring day so if you gentlemen will excuse me, I must retire to my bed." Adding with a benign smile. "After such a copious meal, and with Lieutenant Blane's fine claret drained to the last drop perhaps you might also consider following my example." The words spoken were more a parental suggestion than an order.

So, on the morning of the fourth of August after allowing his men a late breakfast, seeing the express rider on his way with a dispatch for Sir Jeffrey Amherst, tents were struck, and the little force together with three hundred, and fifty pack-horse and a few cattle continued on their march to Fort Pitt. With Turtle Creek less than two days march away, and not wishing to arrive until the evening, after covering less than a dozen miles much to the delight of the troops who were more used to tramping twice that distance in a day, Colonel Bouquet called a halt.

Early the next morning, with Bushy Run station some twenty miles to the west, filled with a heightened awareness of the dangers lurking ahead of them, Bouquet's little army set off into the surrounding wilderness. All that day, sweltering in the oppressive heat, men and animals slogged along the narrow road. It's torturous route leading them up and down the backs of densely wooded hills, and into the tangled bottoms of hidden valleys. Up ahead, in groups of three and four, the advance guard of Backwoodsmen scouted along both sides of the narrow trail. The remainder, together with a detachment of Highlanders bringing up the rear. With them were Samuel Endicote and his son Adam, every mile taking them deeper into the heartland of those who had murdered their family. Outwardly unchanged by the events that had befallen him, inside Samuel's very being was consumed by hatred. A desire for revenge so strong that it possessed his very soul. Powerless to act alone he had seized on the chance to join Bouquet's army, and although unsure how the enterprise would unfold, given that its sole purpose was to rid the land of heathen savages, he was certain that an opportunity to fulfil his thirst for vengeance would present itself.

Perhaps if he had been among those scouting the woods up ahead, and he had possessed the eyesight of a hawk, unwittingly he might have glimpsed the cause of this hatred. Seen for himself, the person responsible for this murderous desire for revenge which plagued his life. But sadly, even if he had set eyes on Shingas he would never have known that the person he was looking at was to blame for the events which had blighted his life. Except for the undisputable fact that the murderer's had been Indians, and most likely Mingos, their identity was a mystery to him. But none of this mattered to him now, his only wish was to kill as many red devils as fate brought before him. Whether it was with his musket or hatchet or his own bare hands he cared little for who they were or what tribe they belonged to. Only when all were sent to hell would he find relief from the agony of his loss.

Equally unaware of the farmer's presence, looking down from their vantage point, concealed by dense foliage Shingas and a group of Seneca warriors, their faces daubed with fresh war paint watched as the column of soldiers made their way towards them through the verdant forest. Like a snake moving through tall grass. Having seen enough, turning away, Shingas and his warriors melted away into the trees.

Riding at the head of the column, flanked by several of his officers, after a tiring day in the saddle Colonel Bouquet finally received the welcome news that Bushy Run station was less than half a mile away. With a shout of thanks to the Backwoodsman who had brought him word, turning his horse he began riding back along the column of weary soldiers. Calling out to them in a cheery voice as he trotted past.

"A few yards more my lads, and you shall have the rest you deserve."

The words sweet music to the weary soldiers who, burdened down by their heavy muskets, had foot-slogged for twenty miles cursing and sweating in the sweltering heat. But no sooner had the words escaped his lips when from up ahead came the rattle of gunfire and mingled in with it the unmistakable sound of Indian war cries.

With the column halted on the crest of a low hill, shouting out a command Colonel Bouquet ordered Lieutenant McIntosh with two Light Infantry companies from the 42nd regiment forward to support the advance guard. Watching anxiously as they disappeared into the woods. Within a few minutes his fears were realized as rather than dropping away, the sound of musket fire increased. Drawn up behind him, grim-faced the soldiers and drivers listened with growing concern as the sounds of battle grew louder. With his thoughts in order, calmly gathering his mounted officers around him Colonel Bouquet issues his orders. With his instructions received, wheeling his horse Lieutenant Graham called out to the two companies of Grenadiers at the head of the line, ordering them to deploy as flankers alongside the supply convoy. No sooner had they broken ranks when the imposing figure of Major Campbell, mounted on his big grey horse began forming the remaining troops into an extended line. Bellowing out the order to fix bayonets at the top of his voice.

Up ahead unable to advance or retreat, with the dead and wounded lying where they had fallen the advance guard of Backwoodsmen, and Highlanders supported by the two companies of Light Infantry found themselves pinned down by heavy gunfire. Finding what cover they could among the scattered trees they returned fire. The Backwoodsmen chose to pick their target when one presented itself. While in time-honored tradition Lieutenant McIntosh's companies responded with coordinated volleys, which invariably spattered harmlessly among the trees. Fearing for their lives, just as the enemy's fire intensified, suddenly a solid line of Highlanders and Grenadiers charged out from the trees behind them. Their mounted officers, swords raised urging them on.

Concealed behind trees and bushes Shingas and a hundred or so warriors watched as the line of soldiers clambered up the sloping ground towards them. Their scarlet uniforms conspicuous among the verdant foliage. Their naked bayonets glinting in the occasional shafts of sunlight. Choosing their moment, leaping from cover they poured a heavy fire into the advancing soldiers. Watching with satisfaction as the line of soldiers wilted under the wasting volley. The gaps in the ranks quickly filled. The wild Highlanders among them screaming out like Banshees. Without time to reload their muskets, and the line of soldiers advancing steadily towards them, abandoning their positions Shingas and his warriors melted away into the woods. With the ridge cleared of the enemy, a great cheer went up from Highlanders and

Grenadiers alike, and the charge was brought to a halt. But even as they celebrated their success, from their rear came the crash of musket fire accompanied by the shriek of war cries. Fearing that the convoy would be lost, and with nothing to be gained by pursuing such an elusive enemy, Bouquet gave the order to fall back.

With his warriors crowded around him, their muskets reloaded, impatient to renew the fight Shingas watched with satisfaction as the soldiers began their withdrawal. Judging the moment, leaping to his feet with a guttural cry he charged down the sloping hills. His warriors bounding along behind him like bloodhounds freed from the leash, emptying their muskets into the ranks of retreating soldiers.

With the supply train under his command, to make it easier for the two companies of Grenadiers to defend it, Lieutenant Graham began urging the drivers to coral their strings of packhorses. No sooner had they begun to comply with his wishes when the rattle of gunfire erupted on both sides. A storm of bullets striking men and horses alike. Unperturbed by the ensuing panic among the drivers, pistol in hand Graham quickly ordered his Grenadiers to form into ranks along both flanks of the convoy. Watching with satisfaction as with practiced ease, the soldiers took up their position. With their muskets ready, the young officer shouted out his order, his voice ringing out above the din. The Grenadier's muskets exploded in a deafening volley.

Up ahead, following their Colonel's orders, begrudgingly the Grenadiers and Highlanders, some of them supporting a wounded comrade, began falling back towards the beleaguered supply column. Shingas and his warriors snapping at their heels like a pack of hungry wolves. Scalping the dead and dying soldiers left behind and stripping them of their weapons.

As the first officer to emerge from the forest, the bullet hole in the sleeve of his scarlet uniform a testimony to his good fortune, surrounded by a body of Highlanders, raising his sword aloft Major Campbell spurred his horse towards the hard-pressed

Grenadiers. Needing little in the way of encouragement, yelling at the tops of their voices to a man the Highlanders charged after him their bayonets thirsty for blood. Seeing the kilted soldiers running towards them and knowing they would quickly be outnumbered Pahotan called his warriors away. Those with muskets firing a ragged volley into the ranks of Grenadiers before melting away into the trees.

With the supply convoy safe from immediate danger, and thankful for the lack of a sustained attack by their savage enemies, Bouquet's soldiers began securing an area of the hillside as protection for the packtrain, and its terrified animals. Grenadiers, Highlanders and the Light Infantry standing shoulder to shoulder in a ring of steel. At its center, seemingly oblivious to being fired on from all directions, stripping the hundreds of flourbags from the packhorses a party of Backwoodsmen began building a low barricade. A defensive position but also a sanctuary for the wounded soldiers.

Galled, Shingas watched as Bouquet's soldiers began organizing themselves into a defensive ring. Angry that the combined force of Seneca, Delaware and Shawnee had not pressed home with the attack while the enemy were unprepared. But without an overall commander, each tribe being led by their war chief, and lacking a coherent strategy, the opportunity had been missed. But all was not lost, for although equal in number Shingas knew that his enemy was not used to this type of warfare. Being more accustomed to the European method of fighting their battles in open fields. Where opposing armies, each resplendent in their colorful uniforms, standards unfurled, the booming of cannon in their ears faced each other in extended ranks. Not for them this wilderness of forest and hills with an enemy lurking behind every tree. The tactics of strike and run were something they had yet to embrace. And this he hoped might prove to be their downfall.

With the day only half done, even as the party of Backwoodsmen labored over the walls of flour bags, Pahotan and a combined force of Seneca and Delaware warriors were moving unseen through the crowded trees. At Pahotan's side was a Delaware war chief named Custaloga, his long, black flowing hair crested with raven feathers, his cheeks daubed with vermilion and ochre. Resting lightly in the hollow of his arm was a fearsome war club. Up ahead of them, glimpsed through the crowded trees the thin line of soldiers guarding the lower slope waited anxiously.

Sensing a lull in the battle, with the protective wall of flour bags erected, Bouquet issued the order for the more seriously wounded to be removed from the line. The remainder, including those with a minor wound, remaining at their post. Behind them, their ears pricked, nostrils flared, the herd of horses and cattle milled around nervously, their drivers struggling to keep the terrified animals in check.

Close to the crest of the hill, with a good view to their front Samuel and half a dozen Backwoodsmen settled themselves in behind a fallen tree. Each man eagerly awaiting the chance to send a musket ball into any savage foolish enough to show himself. Following his father's instructions Adam remained behind the protective wall of flour bags, the wounded stretched out on the ground around him passive and helpless. He had wanted to stay by his father's side but having already lost three of his four sons to these heathen devils Samuel was not about to let them take the last of them.

Then suddenly the silence was shattered by a war cry and pouring a murderous volley into the line of soldiers, whooping and yelling Custaloga and his Delaware warriors burst out from the surrounding forest. Determined to engage the enemy at close quarters, with Captain Bassett at their head a dozen soldiers with fixed bayonets charged forward. But even as they broke ranks, Custaloga and his warriors were already melting away into the deeper woods, their copper-skinned bodies acting as natural camouflage. Frustrated by the Indian's tactics, no sooner had Captain Bassett and his men returned to their position when breaking cover, Pahotan and his Seneca braves opened fire, sending a hail of missiles into them. With a musket ball lodged in his shoulder,

Captain Graham dropped to his knees. Beside him a Grenadier slumped to the ground, a feathered shaft protruding from his left eye. A fellow soldier stepping forward to take his place, filling the gap in the ranks. Enraged by the audacity of the attack, screaming as loud as any Highlander, flanked by men of the Light Infantry Captain Bassett charged forward. Behind him, willing hands removed the dead and dying from the line.

With the Indians pressing home their attack from all sides, crouching behind their barricade Samuel and the Backwoodsmen began firing at will. Each man taking pleasure in seeing their shot strike home. Hidden behind the wall of sack, the bodies of the wounded lying around him bandaged and bleeding terrified Adam pressed himself into a corner of the makeshift wall. His hands clamped over his ears to shut out their plaintive cries for water.

After fighting without respite for over seven hours, with night's inky darkness as arbiter the firing from both sides gradually subsided and eventually dropped away to an uneasy silence as the exhausted soldiers, desperate for rest slumped to the ground where they stood. The officers moving amongst them praising them for their discipline and steadfast resolve. Fearful of lighting fires, with what few supplies they had distributed among the weary defenders, the camp settled into an uneasy night. The soldier's fitful sleep occasionally broken by a wild yell from the forest. A reminder of what awaited them once the cloak of darkness was lifted.

With the camp secured, and sentries posted at intervals around its perimeter Colonel Bouquet retired to the small tent which had been erected for him alongside the barricade of flour bags. Conscious of the hardships awaiting them the following day, and the very real prospect that none of them may survive, aided by the light of a guttering candle he began writing of the day's events, and his fears for tomorrow in a dispatch to Sir Jeffrey Amherst. Concluding with a report on the day's casualties together with a commendation for the gallantry of the officers and men under his command. Written in the hope that even if all were to perish, a truthful chronicle of events might somehow find its way into Sir Jeffrey's possession.

We also suffered considerably: Lieutenant. Graham and Lieutenant James McIntosh of the 42nd are killed and Capt. Graham wounded. Of the Royal American Regt. Lieut. Dow is shot through the body. Of the 77th Lieutenant Donald Campbell and Mr. Peebles, a volunteer, are wounded. Our loss of men, including Backwoodsmen and drivers, exceeds sixty killed or wounded. The action lasted from one O"clock "till night and we expect to begin again at daybreak. Whatever our fate may be, I thought it necessary to give your Excellency this early information, that you may at all events, take such measures as you will think proper with the Provinces, for their own safety and the effectual relief of Fort Pitt, as in case of another engagement I fear insurmountable difficulties in protecting and transporting our provisions, being already so much weakened by the losses of the day, in men and horses: besides the additional necessity of carrying the wounded, whose situation is truly deplorable.

I cannot sufficiently acknowledge the constant assistance I have received from Major Campbell during the long action; nor express my admiration for the cool and steady behavior of the troops, who did not fire a shot without orders and drove the enemy from their posts with fixed bayonets. The conduct of the Officers is much above my praises.

I have the Honor to be, with great respect, Sir & ca.
Henry Bouquet.

Awoken by the sound of a dawn chorus such as they had never heard before, the soldiers climbed wearily to their feet. The deafening crash of muskets and the war cries of their savage enemy ringing in their ears. Seeking what cover, they could find against the hail of deadly missiles they calmly awaited the expected assault. They didn't have long to wait.

At the foot of the low hill, clambering over the trunks of fallen trees, concealed by the evergreen foliage Shingas and a large body of Seneca and Shawnee warriors moved towards the thin line of troops. Closing to within fifty feet, levelling their muskets, they poured a heavy fire into defenders. Then, partially obscured by the clouds of musket smoke, the stench of gunpowder filling the air the warriors charged out from the encircling woods. Brandishing their tomahawks they fell on their enemy, hacking at the wounded laying helpless on the ground, and forcing back the hard-pressed survivors.

Witnessing the potential breach in their line of defense, supported by a company of Highlands, held in reserve for such an eventuality, a sword in his hand Captain Bassett charged down the slope towards the beleaguered soldiers. With blood dripping from his axe, alerted by the battle cries of the Highlanders, shouting out a warning to his warriors Shingas began backing away towards the safety of the trees. His warriors, many of them clutching a bloody trophy following close on his heels. Those with a loaded musket firing a parting shot at the advancing Highlanders.

No sooner had Bassett and his Highlanders filled the breach in the defensive circle when from every side, parties of Shawnee and Delaware warriors rushed forward. Falling with ever-increasing ferocity on the defenders. Determined to break through the ranks of the soldiers. Within the camp itself, terrified by the shrieks and yells of the Indians, small groups of pack horses began breaking free from the milling herd, and bursting through the ring of troops they raced away into the encircling forest.

Enraged by the sight of the fleeing animals, oblivious to the bullets flying around him, Major Campbell strode across to where a group of drivers were cowering against the wall of sacks. Bellowing out to them to control their animals. But his words fell on deaf ears. Many simply chose to ignore him while others, unarmed and helpless, ran off seeking what cover they could find among the trees and bushes. Turning away in disgust, as he made his way to where his mount was securely tethered, the horse suddenly

166

dropped to its knees when it was struck in the head by a stray musket ball. Its life snuffed out in an instant.

All morning the fight raged on, and despite being wearied by fatigue and thirst, having been without water, save for what remained in their canteens since the previous morning the battle-weary troops maintained their defensive circle around the convoy. Observing the battle from his position at the heart of the camp, seeing the growing number of his gallant soldiers falling in their ranks, Colonel Bouquet sensed the tide of battle was turning against them. Determined to reverse their fortunes, gathering his officers around him, with bullets droning past like angry bees in a rising voice, he informed them of his plan.

"Gentlemen, I fear gallantry alone will not win us this fight. Indeed, if all is not to be lost the savages must be made to stand their ground and fight."

Silently, the ring of grim-faced officers nodded their agreement.

"And since from want of numbers, we cannot attack them, lest we place our wounded in great danger. I intend a strategy to bring the enemy to us. On my command Major Campbell", he continued, a note of urgency in his voice, "you are to withdraw a company of Light Infantry, and a company of Highlanders from the 42nd from the line. The troops on each flank will then be required to pull back, and close ranks to fill the gap. It is my hope that the Savages will mistake this maneuver as a sign that we intend to retreat and become so filled with confidence that they will attack us in force. You and your men are then to take up a position to the left of the line where the enemy cannot observe you, and if the strategy is successful, choosing the most auspicious moment you are to fall upon their right flank. Is that understood?"

Fixing Bouquet with his dark hooded eyes Major Campbell nodded his head. "You, Sir", Bouquet went on, turning to face Captain Bassett, "with the Third Light Infantry Company and the Grenadiers of the 42nd will take up such a position that at the first favorable moment you can add your support to the attack." Adding with a last look at the circle of faces surrounding him. "I fear that we shall only have one chance at it gentlemen so strike them hard, and show no mercy."

Sword in hand, calmly issuing his orders Major Campbell began withdrawing the two companies from the line. While at the same time, complying with their colonel's wishes, his two Lieutenants began pulling back the troops on both flanks until the breach left by the withdrawing troops was filled. In the meantime, out of sight of their enemy Captain Bassett, and the companies of Light Infantry and Grenadiers began moving towards their allotted position. A shallow depression between two low hills which overlooked the right flank of Major Campbell's force. Once in position, the naked steel of their bayonets glinting in the shafts of morning sunlight, they awaited the outcome of Colonels Bouquet's audacious plan.

From the encircling forest, Pahotan and Custaloga watched with mounting interest as the soldiers began withdrawing from their position. Slowly retreating towards the center of the camp. With so few soldiers left to oppose them, filled with confidence, the two war chiefs signaled to their waiting warriors, drawing them closer. Moments later, after pouring a volley of musket fire and arrows into the thin line of soldiers, a hundred Seneca and Delaware warriors armed with tomahawks and war clubs charged out from the trees their chilling war cries resounding through the forest.

Overwhelmed by the ferocious assault, their meagre wall of bayonets little protection against the Indian's savage onslaught, the badly outnumbered soldiers were slowly forced back. Their dead and wounded left to the mercy of the scalping knife. With the line breached, eager to put their hated enemy under the knife until not a single soldier was left alive the Seneca and Delaware Braves pressed forward.

Concealed by a low ridge, Major Campbell watched with growing satisfaction as the enemy swallowed the bait. Confident that the time was right, advancing the companies of Light Infantry and Highlanders to the crest of the low ridge, allowing them a moment to level their muskets and take aim he roared out. "Fire!" Instantly, a crashing volley echoed through the trees, the deadly hail of musket balls scythed into the unsuspecting Indians. Stunned by the surprise attack, with dozens killed or wounded the surviving Seneca and Delaware warriors turned to face the new danger. Watching in horror, as consumed with frustration at having to endure a battle fought under conditions imposed on them by their elusive enemy, given a chance to take the fight to the enemy the two companies of Infantry began charging down the slope towards them.

Screaming defiantly, Pahotan turned to face the onrushing soldiers. Recovering from the suddenness of the attack, following his example, with tomahawks and war clubs at the ready the remaining warriors prepared to meet the soldier's onslaught. But the shock was too much. The soldier's bayonets were too irresistible, and after a brief resistance, with panic spreading through the surviving warriors like flames through dry grass they turned and fled. Caught up in the ensuing melee, instinctively, Pahotan lashed out at the soldier in front of him with his hatchet. Its steelhead burying itself into the man's face, the sharpened blade slicing through cartilage and bone, and dropping him onto his knees. Freeing his axe, shouting out his war-cry Pahotan turned to face his next assailant. But even as he caught sight of the soldier it was already too late, and with a primeval yell, the Highlander, a blood-stained bandage wound around his head plunged his bayonet deep into the war chief's chest. The violent impact of the thrust dropping him onto his knees. Wrenching the blade free, his face contorted with hatred, the soldier lunged forward again, driving the bloodied bayonet into Pahotan's exposed throat.

With the din of battle ringing in his ears, leading his men to the crest of the low hill overlooking Major Campbell's flank, Captain Bassett quickly formed them into two ranks. No sooner had the soldiers taken station when dozens of fleeing Indians suddenly appeared directly in front of them. Seizing the moment, the officers shouted out his command. Watching with grim satisfaction as many of the savages, caught in the heavy volley suddenly tumbled to the ground.

From his vantage point, confronted by the unbroken defensive ring of soldiers, powerless to go to their aid Shingas watched helplessly as the surviving Seneca and Delaware warriors fled into the woods. Knowing that the battle was lost, without allowing the bitterness of defeat to manifest itself, gathering his band of Seneca warriors about him Shingas slipped away into the sanctuary of the forest.

With the camp secured, and their enemy defeated the exhausted soldiers slumped to the ground. Barely able to muster up the strength for a rousing cheer in celebration at the appearance of their victorious comrades, back from their pursuit of the Indians. Two of the returning Highlanders had managed to capture one of the fleeing savages and dragging him forward they threw the unfortunate prisoner onto the ground in front of the assembled troops. A great cheer going up as pistol in hand Major Campbell strode forward and calmly raising his weapon, he dispatched the hapless warrior. Shooting him through the head as though he were putting down a rabid dog.

With the woods cleared of the enemy, eager to move on to the station at Bushy Run where men and horses could, at last, relieve their thirst, after giving instruction for litters to be prepared for the dead and the wounded, and any bags of flour which couldn't be transported to be burned, Colonel Bouquet again put pen to paper. A dispatch to his Commanding Officer informing him in concise terms of the day's events while speaking modestly of his own part in the victory. Sighting the losses among his force during the two days of battle as eight officers and one hundred and fifteen men killed, he would leave the unenviable task of listing their names and rank deferred until a more opportune time. Concluding as always with praise for the valor displayed by his troops.

That on this occasion, their behavior speaks for itself so strongly that for me to attempt to eulogize further, would but detract from their merit.

CHAPTER TWELVE

With the safety of Fort Pitt secured, reinforced by a force of a thousand provincial troops, raised and authorized by the Pennsylvania Assembly, determined to punish those tribes responsible for the attacks on His Majesties forts, and the western settlements, and to subjugate them utterly Colonel Bouquet began making his plans for the forthcoming campaign. A venture which would take him into a wilderness where no English army had ever set foot before. And while ratified by necessity it was also an enterprise fraught with danger.

So, in early October with the remnants of his regulars well rested, bolstered by a force of Provincial Levies, and those backwoodsmen who had chosen to remain, with his supplies loaded onto packhorses, and sufficient cattle and sheep to provide meat for the journey Colonel Bouquet set off on his march of retribution. Crossing the Allegheny River, without a road of any sort to follow, scores of engineers and axe men, brought along for the task set to hacking a path through the wall of trees. Ahead of them the Backwoodsmen, men whom Colonel Bouquet now held in high regard following their prowess at Bushy Run, scouting the forest for signs of danger. Day after day the army toiled through the seemingly unending wilderness of dark woods and tangled thickets. Making at best little more than eight miles a day, slowly but inexorably it made its way down the Ohio valley. Each man, soldier or frontiersman marveling at the majestic vistas of forest and mountain as they ventured deeper into the heartland of their enemy.

Occasionally they would encounter the broad expanse of the Ohio River and where possible they would follow its slowly eddying current. Enjoying the brightness of the grassy margins along its wide shoreline, each dotted with groves of maple and basswood. On the tenth day of their march, they reached the banks of the Muskingum River, and after following its serpentine course for several miles, finding a suitable fording place they crossed over to the western bank and made camp.

Setting off the next morning, a party of Indians were spotted skulking around the edges of the surrounding woods. Quickly slipping away when Major Campbell seated astride his new mount, and a party of Highlanders advanced towards them. Continuing down the wooded valley of the Muskingum, on the second day they came across an abandoned Tuscarora village, and while there was hardly any need to broadcast the arrival of his troops, seizing the opportunity to increase the Indian's fears, much to his men's delight, Colonel Bouquet ordered them to burn it to the ground. The tell-tale clouds of black smoke rising above the treetops, a sign of his impending arrival.

The following day, reaching a spot where a wide meadow offered grazing for his animals, and where an adequate supply of firewood could be obtained from the surrounding woodland Colonel Bouquet ordered a halt. Eager to create a more permanent camp, axe men were soon at work felling trees for the construction of a wooden palisade where their stores, and animals could be securely housed. While elsewhere groups of soldiers were soon busy erecting rows of tents and digging fire-pits. Every man spurred on by the sight of the butchers going about their work, and the cooks laying out their utensils in preparation for the evening meal. Satisfied that everything was in hand, with late afternoon approaching Colonel Bouquet assembled his officers, and after thanking them for their efforts he gave orders for the twenty Mohawk Indians, sent to him as guides and interpreters by Sir William Johnson, to be dispatched to the surrounding villages of the Shawnee and Delaware. Their mission was to give instructions to the tribal chiefs that under pain of death they were to attend a meeting with him the following day on the meadow bordering the river below their encampment.

With a watery sun blessing the occasion with its presence, accompanied by the rattle of drums Colonel Bouquet's troops moved in formation onto the meadow. Their heavy boots tramping down the dew-laden grass. The polished blades of their bayonets glinting in the brightening light. Standing its center was a rustic arbor, constructed the previous day from saplings, and wooden boughs. Seated beneath it on chairs carried from Fort Pitt for such an occasion, Colonel Bouquet and his senior officers looked on with pride as the soldiers formed up in front of them in extended lines. The bare-legged Highlanders in their tartan kilts on one side, the Royal Americans in their scarlet coats on the other. With a single rank of Provincial Levies in their dull blue jackets, and red waistcoats together with a somewhat disorderly line of Backwoodsmen in their fringed hunting shirts enclosing the arbor on both sides. A display of military might clearly, intended to impress their enemy while also striking fear into their hearts.

With the sun climbing higher in the sky, after an anxious wait a delegation of tribal chiefs surrounded by a crowd of warriors appeared on the far bank of the Muskingum River. A much-relieved Colonel Bouquet and his officers watched as a small fleet of canoes began ferrying them across the wide expanse of water. Once ashore, walking in a single file, the tribal chiefs made their way towards the arbor. At the head of the small procession, dressed in all their finery, a colored blanket draped around their shoulders were Custaloga and Kiashuta. Their bold features painted with ochre, vermilion, white lead and soot. If they were meant to be impressed by the show of arms, their haughty, impervious expressions revealed little sign of it.

With one exception the members of the delegation seated themselves cross-legged on the blankets laid out on the ground in front of the hated English officers. The one who had remained standing stepped forward, and handing Bouquet a lighted pipe. Watching as it was passed from officer to officer. Each of them drawing in a mouthful of smoke before passing it to the person seated beside him. With the ceremony completed, returning the pipe to the elderly chief Bouquet watched impatiently as the process was repeated among the seated Indians. Finally, with the ritual concluded, a Delaware chief named Turtle Heart slowly climbed to his feet, a beaded bag clutched in one of his gnarled hands, and pulling himself erect he began addressing the officers seated before him. Pausing at relevant moments in his speech to remove a string of colored shells woven into a belt and handing them to

Colonel Bouquet. His grasp of English, both admirable and eloquent.

"Brothers", he began, his voice surprisingly youthful, "I speak on behalf of the nations present before you, and with these tokens, I open your ears and your hearts so that you may listen to my words." Brothers, this war was neither, our fault nor yours but the work of those nations who live to the west, and their wild young men who would have killed us had we not done their bidding. Brothers, you come amongst us with the hatchet raised to strike us. We now take it from your hand and throw it away. My brothers, it is the will of the Great Spirit that there should be peace between us. We on our side now take hold of the chain of friendship but as we cannot hold it alone, we desire that you will also take hold, and never let it fall from our hands again. Brothers these words come from our hearts, not our lips." Concluding his address with a final act of subjugation. "You ask us to return to you all the prisoners amongst us and this we will do. All we ask is that we are given time to do this thing."

With his lengthy speech concluded, pulling his blanket about him Turtle Heart seated himself cross-legged on the ground. No sooner was he seated when one after the other, each chief followed suit. All voicing their agreement in words the officers had no understanding of before presenting Bouquet with a belt of beaded wampum together with a small bundle of sticks. The latter an indication of the number of prisoners held by them, and who they promised to give up.

With the last of the tokens placed before him, Colonel Bouquet climbed to his feet. His normally benign manner replaced by feelings of resentment, and anger at the hypocrisy displayed by the Indians. Dispensing with the usual form of address at such meetings with its implied overtones of friendship, choosing instead a more formal approach, he began his response. The sound of his voice was carrying to the ranks of assembled soldiers. His words, music to their ears.

"Sachems, War-Chiefs, the excuses you have offered us are both frivolous and unavailing, and your conduct is without defense or apology. Your warriors attacked our forts, built with your consent, and you treacherously destroyed our outposts at Venango and Le Boeuf. Your warriors also assailed our troops, the same troops who now stand before you, in the woods at Bushy Run. The same." Pausing in mid-sentence, at the sudden appearance of a young Delaware maiden, her liquid brown eyes staring at him questioningly. Unsure as to how he should respond to this unforeseen interruption, before he had time to react, averting her eyes she walked across to Custaloga and seating herself close beside him, she began whispering into his ear. Quickly translating the officer's words into her native tongue. Recognizing her role in the proceedings, allowing the young woman to finish, Bouquet then continued with his address. His tone of voice emphatic, his words uncompromising.

"We shall endure this no longer and I have now come amongst you to force you to make atonement for the injuries you have done to us." said Bouquet, his gaze lingering on the Delaware maiden. Smiling to himself as the chief's eyes began burning with anger as she relayed his words.

"Your allies the Ottawa, Ojibwas and Wyandots have begged for peace, even The Six Nations have leagued themselves with us. The great lakes and rivers around you are all in our possession. Even your friends the French are subject to our will and can do no more to aid you." Concluding in a rising voice. "You are all in our power, and if we choose, we can exterminate you from the earth."

Filled with terror by the sternness of his words, their faces as imperturbable as always, the Chiefs listened with growing alarm. After waiting a moment for the gravity of his words to sink in, Colonel Bouquet continued. His tone a bit softer now. His words more accommodating. "But the English are a merciful and generous people and were it possible for you to convince us that you sincerely repent of your past acts. That we could depend on your good behavior for the future then you might yet hope for mercy and peace." Then, extending his arms in a benevolent gesture. "If I find that you have faithfully executed the conditions, which I shall prescribe I will not treat you with the severity you deserve. I will give you twelve days from now to deliver into my hands all the prisoners in your possession, without exception. Men, women and children whether adopted into your tribes, married or living among you under any denomination or pretense whatsoever. Furthermore, you are to furnish them with clothing and provisions sufficient to carry them back to their settlements. When you have complied with these conditions you shall then learn on what terms you may obtain the peace you desire." Adding as a final reminder of his supremacy. "As proof of your intentions, I shall require three of your principal chiefs to be given as hostages as security that you will preserve good faith."

With the significance of Bouquet's words made known to him, Custaloga leapt to his feet, his hand reaching under his blanket for the knife concealed in his belt. But before he could free the blade from its sheath a file of soldiers, their muskets at the ready quickly formed a half-circle around the assembled Chiefs. With a nod from Colonel Bouquet, Custaloga, Kiashuta and a prominent Shawnee chief whose name defied pronouncement, the cold steel of a bayonet pressing against their back, were led away.

Watching as the remaining chiefs filed out from beneath the arbor, his face marred by a frown Colonel Bouquet turned to Captain Bassett seated on the chair next to him.

"Alas, for all their fine words I fear that they may yet need some persuasion before my conditions are met." His tone of voice conveying a sense of disappointment.

"Perhaps sir, given your misgivings might not a search of some of their villages provide the necessary encouragement for those who are reluctant to carry out your wishes?" Captain Bassett replied, seizing on his commanding officer's lack of optimism, and the opportunity it presented.

After pondering the suggestion for a moment, seeing no obvious disadvantages to it, Colonel Bouquet nodded his head.

"Very well captain", said Bouquet, well aware of the officer's eagerness for action. "As you say perhaps a show of arms may well dispel any thoughts of leniency they may harbor."

With a broad smile lighting up his face. Eager to escape the confines of inactivity, throwing up his arm in a salute Captain Bassett turned on his heels, and strode away. His stride lengthening with every step.

CHAPTER THIRTEEN

The moment Captain Bassett rode into the village at the head of two companies of red-coated Light Infantry, the old woman knew instantly what she must do, and taking hold of Esther's hand, she hurried away. Once inside the long-house, putting a finger to her lips she pointed to one of the cots. Aware of the old woman's intentions with the sleeping infant clutched in her arms Esther climbed on the cot. The old woman quickly covered them with a blanket of furs. Satisfied that both were well hidden, praying that they would not be discovered she turned and walked away.

Reaching the quadrangle, his excited horse dancing under him, Captain Bassett gazed imperviously at the gathering crowd of Indians. A mixture of fear and astonishment etched onto every face. With the two infantry companies drawn up before him, shouting out in a loud voice, he gave the order for them to begin a thorough search of the village. Watching in anticipation after dividing into pairs, the soldiers began making their way towards the encircling long houses.

Concealed under the blanket of furs, her baby son cradled in her arms Esther listened as someone entered the longhouse. The sound of their heavy footsteps as they made their way down the central aisle quickly identifying them as soldiers. Hardly daring to breathe, fearing that at any moment the baby might awake Esther listened as they drew nearer. The sound of their voices, although indistinct, grew louder as they moved from room to room.

Muskets in hand, the two soldiers made their way down the center of the long-house searching each compartment in turn but without any great conviction. Prodding half-heartedly here and there with their bayonets and smashing a few earthenware pots with their heavy boots. Grumbling aloud at having to carry out such a menial task. Especially when back at Fort Pitt their fellow soldiers were having such an easy time of things. This was the third village they had searched since setting out a week ago, and their enthusiasm for the task had long since evaporated. Finally, satisfied that they had done enough to show they had carried out their orders, the pair made their way back along the aisle. Once outside, thankful for leaving the building's gloomy interior, they began making their way towards the next long-house.

Sitting astride his horse Captain Bassett watched in anticipation as his troops moved from long-house to long-house searching for prisoners. Although they had nothing to show for their efforts so far, nevertheless he was enjoying being out in the field, soldiering again. Remaining at Fort Pitt and playing nursemaid to a host of frightened settlers was not something which held any great appeal for him. Gathered around him, the large crowd of Seneca, old and young, looked on in anxious silence. There were only a few warriors in evidence, standing apart from the crowd their sullen expressions betraying their hatred of the red-coated soldiers.

Having positioned herself in the forefront of the encircling crowd, unlike the other onlookers Meeataho was delighted by the arrival of the soldiers. The reason for their presence filling her with pleasure. Soon the Yengeese woman would be gone. Taken away, and returned to her people, and then Shingas would be hers. With the thought thrilling in her chest, Meeataho waited anxiously for the two soldiers to emerge from the white woman's long house with their prize.

Moments later her hopes were turned to dust as she watched in disbelief as the two soldiers emerged from the long-house empty-handed. Consumed by anger and frustration, pushing aside those in front of her Meeataho rushed across the quadrangle towards the mounted figure of Captain Bassett. Avoiding the dancing hooves of his skittish horse, gesturing with her arm towards the longhouse the two soldiers had emerged from, Meeataho began shouting at him. Perplexed, Captain Bassett looked down at her. The woman was clearly distraught, but he had no idea why, or indeed what she was trying to tell him with her infernal gibberish. In an attempt to resolve matters, he called out to the Mohawk warrior who had been brought along as an interpreter.

"You there, what is she saying? Ask her what she wants of me?"

Acknowledging the officer's wishes, walking across to where Meeataho was standing the Mohawk warrior spoke to her. Listening, emotionless, as she repeated what she had said to the English officer.

"She, say white woman in cabin."

"Can, she be sure?" said Bassett, a little perplexed by the suggestion.

"She sure." The warrior replied, slowly nodding his head.

Intrigued by the possibility that what the woman was saying might be true, turning in his saddle Captain Bassett called out to one of his NCOs.

"Sergeant, go and search that building." Pointing to the longhouse in question. "Thoroughly this time, do you hear?"

Not at all pleased by being asked to carry out a task normally assigned to lower ranks, reluctantly, the NCO made his way to the long house and pulling aside the curtain, he ducked inside.

Gripped by a sense of anticipation, the villagers focused their gaze on the doorway. Minutes later the NCO reappeared and holding back the curtain, with her infant clutched to her chest, Esther emerged into the bright sunlight. Expectantly, a murmur rippled through the crowd. Allowing her a moment to compose herself, taking Esther gently by the arm the sergeant escorted her across to the mounted officer.

Delighted that his quest had at last born fruit, making an effort to replace the self-satisfied smile on his face with one of benevolence Captain Bassett looked down on the face of the woman staring up at him.

"Don't be afraid, you're safe now. Your ordeal is over."

Overcome with emotion, unable to speak Esther simply gazed up at the British Officer resplendent in his scarlet jacket.

"What is your name?" Asked Bassett, a little put out by the woman's apparent indifference at being found. "Can you remember what you are called?"

Struggling at first to find the words, eventually, Esther found her voice.

"Esther Colwill. I am called Esther Colwill."

Smiling ingeniously, Captain Bassett fixed his gaze on the hybrid infant cradled in her arms.

"And the child, is it yours?"

"Yes", Esther replied. Taken aback by the question. "Yes, the child is mine."

"And its father, is he here?" Bassett asked, gesturing towards the group of warriors. "Can you point him out?"

Shocked by his words, Esther clutched the infant to her protectively.

"Well, have you no answer for me?" Bassett called out, struggling to contain his anger.

"He is not here", Esther replied, terrified by the officer's question.

"Is he dead?"

"I don't know. I . . ."

"Killed while attacking His Majesty's soldiers perhaps?" Bassett shouted, rising out of the saddle.

Shocked, Esther stepped back, the color draining from her face. Standing beside her the sergeant stared up at the officer with undisguised loathing. Catching the look, embarrassed by his show of temper Captain Bassett lowered himself into his saddle.

"No matter. I . . ." His sentence cut short as a young girl suddenly emerged from the crowd of onlookers and came running towards them. Running a gentle hand down his horse's neck, Captain Bassett looked down at the new arrival. His expression softening at the prospect of adding another prisoner to his bounty.

"Well, and who have we here then? Do you have a name child?"

Clinging tightly to Esther's dress, Chantal gazed up at him. More interested in the rows of golden buttons adorning the front of his tunic than in trying to understand what he was saying to her.

"Come now child, surely you can tell me your name", said Bassett, becoming a little impatient.

"She doesn't understand what you are saying." said Esther, squeezing the child's shoulder reassuringly.

Surprised by Esther's comment, Captain Bassett stared at her quizzically.

"She is French", said Esther, by way of an explanation. "A captive like myself."

Stung by Esther's words, Captain Bassett spurred his horse forward.

"Form ranks." He called out loudly. Furious at being made a fool of. Shouting out to the sergeant as he fought to bring the spirited animal under control.

"Set Mistress Colwill and her infant up on one of the packhorses."

"And what of the girl sir?", enquired the NCO. "Are we not to take her too?"

"The girl is French Sergeant she is no concern of ours." Bassett spat back at him, his face as black as thunder.

"No please sir I beg you don't abandon her", cried Esther, horrified by his words. "I will take care of her. I promise she will be no trouble."

"You have your order's Sergeant", Said Bassett, rounding on her. "See that they are carried out."

Knowing that any further protests would be useless, watched by a triumphant Meeataho, Esther allowed herself to be led away. The sight of the old woman walking out from the crowd and making her way towards the wretched figure of Chantel giving her some consolation. A crumb of comfort in knowing that at least the child would have her adoptive grandmother to watch out for her.

CHAPTER FOURTEEN

For two days the broad meadow and surrounding woods resounded to the sound of an axe and saw, and where once there had been acres of grass a good part of it was now occupied by a small town. Encircled by a palisade of sharpened stakes and fortified by wide ditches banked with earth. Behind these defenses, several crude cabins had been constructed to house those prisoners who were without family or relatives until they could be transported back to the settlements in the east. Standing alongside them were several storehouses with a larger building where those requiring the attention of a surgeon-doctor could be treated. Set about them in orderly rows were dozens of white military tents, quarters for the influx of additional troops, which despite its impressive size, the fort was unable to accommodate.

At its heart was a large, open-sided building thirty feet long and almost as wide, its crudely thatched roof supported by the upright trunks of young trees driven into the ground at regular intervals. Its purpose was to act as a meeting house where prisoners brought in by their savage captors could be received by those, hopeful of catching a glimpse of a loved one. A child perhaps, who had been snatched from their bosom, and who they thought had been lost to them forever.

On the twelfth day, as demanded by Bouquet those who were to be repatriated began arriving. A seemingly endless flotilla of birch-bark canoes ferrying them across the wide expanse of the Muskingum River. Reaching the other side, accompanied by their surrogate parents, some with an infant cradled in their arms, captives of differing ages and gender began making their way up the grassy slope towards the meeting house. Running among them like a pack of wild dogs, totally oblivious to the fate which awaited them were troops of half-naked children. Most having been snatched from their natural mothers when they were babies and raised as their own by their adoptive parents. The remainder were mainly young women, many of whom had become the willing partner of an Indian husband. Their hybrid offspring, born in captivity clutched to their breasts.

Awaiting them, crowded together inside the meeting house were dozens of settlers; fathers, mothers, husbands, and brothers all desperately scanning the faces of the approaching captives. As they drew closer, a woman suddenly dashed out from the crowd, and confronting a warrior with a young child in his arms, with a piercing scream she snatched it from him, tears of joy streaming down her face. Instantly, unable to restrain themselves, other settlers surged forward, quickly engulfing the new arrivals. Each of them eagerly searching for a loved one among those being given up.

Bewildered by the presence of so many pale-skinned people, when they were claimed by their natural mothers; a person they had no recollection of, the terrified children simply clung to their adopted parents, unwilling to be parted from them. Also scattered among the prisoners were young women who had been taken as brides. Standing shame-faced when confronted by a father or a brother, many of them holding a baby. Then there were the mothers who had lost their offspring years before, all frantically scanning the faces of the young children in agony of hope and doubt. The cacophony of sobbing and wailing from those who had failed to discover a missing loved one blighting the occasion with their sadness. Deployed around the building the file of battle-hardened soldiers looked on, spectators to the tragic melodrama enfolding before them, their true emotions concealed behind stoic faces.

Wriggling free from the embrace of the woman who had claimed him as her own, the young boy slipped away into the crowd. Weaving a path through the forest of legs as he made his bid for freedom. Spotting the escapee, slinging his musket over his shoulder the watching soldier chased after him. Clear of the meeting house, spurred on by the shouts of his pursuer as he barged his way through the throng of people, the young boy suddenly felt a hand grab him by the arm. Foiled in his bid to escape, looking up he saw the face of Colonel Bouquet smiling down on him. Releasing his captive to the pursuing soldier, with a sense of disquiet Bouquet watched as the soldier made his way back towards the meeting house with the struggling child tucked under his arm like a pig on its way to market. Pushing the thought from his mind, reminding himself of the virtue of his actions with Major Campbell at his side he continued on among the assembled throng of people, the sound of their clamorous voices ringing in his ears.

Reigning in his horse the express rider, the sleeve of his uniform now boasting a corporal's chevron, climbed down from the saddle. Relishing the opportunity to have his feet back on firm ground again, with his mount safely tethered he made his way through the rows of tents. Acquainting himself of the colonel's probable whereabouts from one of the sentries, he made his way towards the meeting house. Being a head taller than most of those around him, he had no trouble in finding Colonel Bouquet among the milling crowd, and with his mail pouch tucked under his arm he shouldered his way towards him.
"A dispatch from Fort Bedford, Sir", said the express rider, saluting as he handed over the document.
"Thank you, corporal", said Bouquet, watching as the express rider removed a document from his pouch.
"Another of Ouray's infernal letters no doubt", said Bouquet turning to face Major Campbell. "I swear the man has ink in his veins for he is forever putting pen to paper, and usually for no other reason than to inform me of events which are of no interest or importance whatsoever."

As the two officers were once more swallowed up by the crowd, with his duty done the express rider turned away, and began making back to his horse. And it was then that he saw them, standing like two lost souls on the fringe of the crowd, their faces etched with despair. Both were dressed as he remembered, and although their appearance had suffered from the rigors of captivity, he recognized them instantly, and with all thoughts of his horse forgotten he made his way towards them.

It was the woman who saw him first. Her hand instinctively flying up to her mouth, suppressing the cry of joy before it could escape her lips. Then the young girl caught sight of him walking towards them, a smile instantly lighting up her sunburnt face. It was the soldier who had ridden up to their cabin on his wonderful bay horse. Better still, he was smiling.

Looking on Adam witnessed their reunion with a pang of regret. Just for a fleeting moment, he had dared to believe that the woman might have been Esther. Disappointed, he turned away drawn by the sound of voices carried up from the river as more canoes began arriving with their cargo of prisoners. Filled with renewed hope that Esther might be among them, he hurried away towards the grassy riverbank.

Content that his demands for the release of their prisoners were being adhered to by the Indians, leaving matters in the hands of Major Campbell Colonel Bouquet began making his way back towards the fort. Passing a small group of captives flanked by stoic warriors, the sight of a settler woman kneeling before a young girl caught his attention. Intrigued, he walked over to her, standing unnoticed among the onlookers. Sensing his presence, the woman looked up at him, tears running down her face.
"She doesn't know me." She wailed, clearly believing the young girl to be her long-lost daughter. "She doesn't know me."
Touched by the woman's plight, Bouquet gazed across at the young girl who from her appearance looked for all the world like an Indian child.
"Forgive me but can you be sure that this child is your own." Bouquet asked, his words tempered by a sympathetic tone of voice.
"I'm as sure as I live and breathe that this child is mine." The woman replied, clearly horrified by his assertion. "The very one as sat on my knee while I sang a lullaby to send her to sleep, I can be sure of that much", she said, wiping at the tears streaming down her cheeks. "She is my own darling daughter, and she has forgotten me."

Touched by her response, leaning down, Colonel Bouquet whispered in her ear.

"Sing the song that you used to sing to her when she was a child."

Bemused at first by his words the woman stared back at him. Then encouraged by the officer's smile, turning to face the young girl she began singing. Instantly, the young girl's face lit up, the words awakening dormant memories, and with a joyful cry, she flung herself into her mother's arms.

Dejected by his fruitless search of the new arrivals Adam trudged back up the slope towards the row of rustic buildings where he and his father had been given temporary lodgings. With his mind on other things, it was purely by chance that he witnessed the arrival of Captain Bassett and his detachment of soldiers as they made their way between the rows of tents. And it was then that he saw her; his Esther riding on the back of one of the packhorses, and his heart leapt. Elated, barging his way through the crowd of people he began running towards her. Wanting to call out to her, the pure enjoyment of seeing her again, the words lodging in his throat. But before he had taken a dozen steps a heavy hand suddenly grabbed him by the shoulder, stopping him in his tracks. Turning, Adam found himself staring at his father.

"Pa it's Esther. I've found her." He cried joyfully, pointing with his arm. "Look there, do you see her?"

Looking towards where his son was pointing, Samuel quickly saw that the lad was right. It was Esther, and even though her hair was in braids, and she was dressed like an Indian her face was unmistakable. But then he saw the infant clutched in her arms, and his expression hardened.

"Best we don't make ourselves known to her just yet." He said, a rough edge to his voice.

In a flash, the smile disappeared from Adam's face.

"But Pa."

"Do as I say now," said Samuel, silencing his protest.

Consumed with disappointment, obediently Adam turned, and walked away. Samuel followed a step behind him, his thoughts alive with possibilities. The discovery of the woman rekindling his hopes for revenge. The possibility that if he was alive, the wolf might come looking for his cub, bringing an uncharacteristic smile to his face.

Having been exiled to the woods while the victorious soldiers searched the surrounding Indian villages, Shingas wolfed down the hot meal. Placing the empty bowl on the cot beside him once he had scraped it clean. As he did so the old woman entered carrying a large pot of freshly heated water. Setting it down at his feet she gazed up at him. Having told him of the fate of his family she knew in her heart that he would not rest until he had found them. She had decided against revealing the part Meeataho had played in their abduction. Content to delay the young maiden's punishment for her treachery until after her family were restored to her. Scooping up the empty bowl, without a word she slipped away, leaving Shingas to his ablutions. With his hunger satisfied reaching into his carry-all Shingas removed a small earthenware jar containing a pale-colored paste. Dipping two fingers into it, he began working the substance onto his face. Rubbing it into the carefully applied design until it resembled an artist's palette. Satisfied, soaking a piece of cloth in the pot of water he began washing off the kaleidoscope of paint. With all evidence of war removed from his face, picking up his musket Shingas left his small compartment. The English redcoats had stolen his family. Now he would take them back.

Seated at the entrance of the makeshift building, with the infant feeding contentedly at her breast, Esther was thankful for what little breeze there was. Behind her other women, some with babies and young children lay stretched out on straw mattresses. Some of them are asleep, others merely seeking some shade. Looking out on the sea of activity before her, Esther caught sight of the young fair-haired boy she had seen running away from the meeting house. Returned to his true family, and clothed in a shirt and breeches, she watched him struggling for all he was worth as they attempted to put his feet into a pair of shoes. Strangely saddened by the scene, as she looked away, there standing as bold as a lion, not twenty paces away was the figure of Shingas. His eyes fixed on her in an unblinking stare. Shocked by his sudden appearance Esther stared back at him, a mixture of emotions flooding her brain. Her heart beating faster as seemingly unconcerned by the presence of the soldier posted at the end of the row, he began walking towards her. Alarmed by the Indian's unwarranted presence the sentry stepped forward his musket held at the ready. Its naked bayonet a warning of intent.

"Halt!" The soldier called out.

Eyeing the sentry with a mixture of hatred and disdain, instinctively Shingas reached for the tomahawk hanging from in his belt. Threatened by the hostile gesture taking a step backwards, the sentry called out.

"Corporal of the guard." His musket levelled at Shingas' chest.

Responding to the sentry's urgent call, a group of armed soldiers began making their way towards the building. Catching sight of them, with his intentions foiled, and not wishing to find himself in chains, Shingas moved away towards the meetinghouse. Quickly losing himself in the milling crowd.

With his hopes realized and his musket in hand Samuel plunged into the throng of people. Adam following close behind him like a faithful hound. Earlier, having seen where the returning soldiers had taken Esther and her infant, he had begun his vigil. Keeping a watch on the building in the hope that if he had survived, the one who had planted his seed in her would come looking for the mother, and her child. Now with his prayers answered, and with the embodiment of his all-consuming hatred revealed to him he would exact his revenge.

With all hope of taking back his family gone, leaving the open meadow, and the unfolding human drama being played out on its grassy stage Shingas slipped away into the surrounding forest. Weaving his way through the crowded trees, it wasn't long before he realized that he was being followed. The sound of his pursuer's heavy footfall was easily discernible in the infinite silence of the woods. Knowing that no Indian would reveal his presence so readily, Shingas continued on his chosen path. Behind him, oblivious to the fact that his quarry was aware of their presence, panting with exertion Samuel lengthened his stride. The overwhelming desire to close the gap between himself and the person he was determined to kill, spurring him on.

Entering the small forest clearing, with his trap sprung, like a trapped animal Shingas turned to confront his pursuers. With less than fifty paces between them, hardly daring to believe his good fortune, throwing up his musket Samuel took aim. Secretly hoping that the musket ball would wound rather than kill, allowing him the chance to finish his victim with the knife. But even as his finger came to rest on the trigger, Cattawa's tomahawk was already flying through the air towards him. Turning end over end, the sound of its whirling flight not unlike the wingbeat of a hundred hummingbirds. Falling silent when its steelhead embedded itself in the middle of Samuel's back, severing his spine.

With a wild yell, pulling his scalping knife from his belt Cattawa raced towards Samuel's prostrate body with his war-cry echoing through the trees. Dropping to his knees he grabbed a handful of his victim's hair but before he could sink the blade into Samuel's flesh, with an enraged roar Adam was on him. And lifting the warrior in his powerful arms, like a petulant child tossing its doll out of its pram, he threw him onto the ground. With his anger absolved, kneeling beside his father's body, oblivious to the dark stain ebbing out from the deep wound in his back he began stroking his hair.

Enraged, Cattawa leapt to his feet, the knife gripped in his hand but before he could move, he found Shingas blocking his path. His hand raised in front of him, the gesture telling the angry warrior that this one was to be spared. Knowing better than to challenge Shingas' authority, sheathing his knife Cattawa stepped away. A sullen expression masking his face as he watched the other members of the small war party crowding around Adam like curious children. Watching him as he rocked gently back and forth, moaning softly through half-open lips. Becoming aware of their presence, with tears running down his cheeks Adam gazed up into their warlike faces. Strangely moved by his pitiful lamentations, taking hold of one of Adam's hands a warrior pulled him onto his feet. And with the war party gathered around him like a protective cloak, like a lost child the last of Samuel Endicote's sons was led away into the forest.

CHAPTER FIFTEEN

Drawn up in line at the edge of the meadow each pulled by a pair of oxen were eight open wagons. Their drivers, whips in hand waited patiently as the last of the unclaimed women, and children climbed aboard in readiness for their journey back to the settlements. Gathered around them were a jostling crowd of Indian women, their faces etched with sorrow at being parted from an adopted daughter-in-law or a child whom they had taken as their own. Each displaying their affection by furnishing them with food and blankets for the long journey ahead.

Seated in the lead wagon, Esther looked down at the distraught women with mixed emotions. Then the baby began crying. It was hungry again. Welcoming the distraction, she unbuttoned her new linen dress, a gift from a kindly settler's wife. She would have no use for it she had cried as she pressed it into Esther's hands. Telling her how she and her husband had come in search of their long-lost daughter but that their quest had been in vain. And while others had begged them not to give up hope, reluctantly, they had resigned themselves to never having her returned to them.

No sooner had the baby begun suckling when a young officer, resplendent in his scarlet jacket, and tricorne hat came galloping across to the line of wagons. Bringing the horse under control he shouted out to the dozen or so soldiers standing a little way off in the shade of the trees. Thankful to be underway at last, shouldering their muskets they made their way across to the wagons, and pushing through the crowd of women they positioned themselves at intervals alongside the small convoy. Happy that the last of those without family were safely aboard, the order was given to proceed and accompanied by the crack of the driver's whips, the line of wagons lumbered away towards the encircling forest.

Thanks in part to the rugged track, recently cleared by the sweated labor of Colonel Bouquet's axe men, with the young officer riding ahead of them the wagons moved along at a steady pace. Slogging along beside them, although not best pleased with their escort duty, the soldiers contented themselves with the prospect of enjoying the pleasures of the alehouse once they reached Carlisle. Seated up in the jolting carts the majority of the women, and children endured their bumpy journey in silence, a few of them exhausted by the events of the past few days dozing off despite the discomfort. Most, whether asleep or awake, especially those with babies, and young children born to them in captivity reflecting on what reception awaited them on their return to civilization.

With the baby asleep in her arms, these thoughts were also uppermost in Esther's mind. Not knowing the fate which had befallen Samuel and Adam, all she could think of was the inevitable reunion with the farmer and his son, and what bearing her capture, and the birth of a child would have in its outcome. Moments later her thoughts were interrupted by a chorus of shrieks from the wagon at the rear. One of its wheels had struck the protruding stump of a tree, dislodging it from its axle, and almost pitching out its terrified occupants. Cursing aloud at his bad luck, climbing down from his seat, assisted by a pair of soldiers, the driver began helping his passengers down from their precarious perch.

With the wagon emptied of its human cargo, removing a stout pole from the bed of the wagon the driver pushed it under the offending axle. Satisfied that it was in position, resting the pole on his shoulder helped by another teamster, the pair attempted to lift the wagon. A third man standing by with the wheel ready to slide it back into place. But even without its load, the weight of the wagon was too much for them. Alerted by the cries of the women, kicking his horse into a run the young officer made his way to the back of the convoy. Seeing the two drivers struggling in vain to raise the wagon, he turned to the group of watching soldiers.

"You men there lend a hand. Look lively now!" He called out, angered by the soldier's reluctance to lend a hand.

With little choice but to obey the officer's order, doing little to disguise their displeasure, setting their muskets aside the three soldiers made their way across to the stricken wagon.

Standing among the passengers who had been helped down from the stricken wagon, the young fair-haired boy glanced around him surreptitiously. Satisfied that everyone, including the escorting soldier's attention, was distracted by the efforts being made to re-fit the wheel to its axle, he began slowly backing away towards the trees. Confident that his absence hadn't been noticed, with a last furtive look he stepped off the track, and ducking under the outstretched branches he slipped away into the forest.

Minutes later, panting for breath the runaway boy burst into the small forest clearing closely followed by three Indian boys all about the same age. United with his boyhood friends, he began stripping off his clothes. Throwing the hated garments onto the ground. The shoes were the last to be removed, the boy taking great delight in hurling them into the trees where they became snagged on the branches. Hanging from the evergreen foliage like some bizarre Christmas decoration. Whooping with joy at his transformation the three Indian boys raced away into the forest. Grinning from ear to ear, as the naked runaway was about to chase after them, he caught sight of Shingas standing on the far side of the clearing. A witness to the boy's audacious escape. A little uncertain, the boy stared back at him. Then, in the blink of an eye reassured by the warrior's silence with a defiant yell, his pale backside flashing like the flag of a fleeing deer, he dashed away into the trees.

As the daylight began to fade, aware of how tiring the day"s journey must have been for his charges, the young officer decided to call a halt. With the large clearing giving sufficient space to accommodate the wagons, after forming them into a defensive square, leaving the teamsters to attend to the needs of their oxen, he set his men to making camp. Stressing the need for a fire to be lit, and a hot meal prepared as a matter of urgency. Whether an oversight or a case of forgetfulness by the fort's quartermaster, it was soon discovered that no tents had been loaded with the provisions. Happily, with little need for privacy, and nothing to fear about the weather with a good supply of blankets, the matter was quickly forgiven and forgotten.

With the camp cloaked in darkness, and everyone fed, after seeing the children settling for the night, most of the returnees took to their beds. Some chose to sleep under the wagons, while others preferred the open ground, and the stars above their heads. After setting a Rota for sentry duty, with one soldier posted on the perimeter of the camp and a second keeping guard on the oxen, and his precious horse, following the teamster's example the young officer climbed into the back of one of the wagons. He expected little trouble from any savages who might be skulking in the woods. Given the severity with which Colonel Bouquet had treated them, and the fearful reprisals they might expect should they misbehave, he doubted any would dare attack the King's soldiers, no matter how small in number. So, content that he had carried out his duty with the hard boards as a mattress, and his saddle as a pillow he quickly fell asleep.

With his back pressed against the scaly bark of the giant Hemlock, stifling a yawn the young soldier stared up at the night sky. Its inky blackness home to a million stars, twinkling above him like a swarm of heavenly fireflies. Resisting the urge to contemplate their origins, or attempt to fathom the mysteries of the universe, instead, he turned his thoughts to the young girl he had become acquainted with during the two days they had spent at Fort Bedford. Pretty as a picture she was with her slender figure, and eyes so deep a person could drown in them. But it was her lips he remembered most. The color of ripe cherries, full and inviting, and although he had never kissed a girl before, the thought of pressing his lips to hers made him feel quite dizzy.

There were others of course who had their eye on her. Older soldiers mostly, courting her attention with their knowing winks, and salacious remarks. But it seemed his shyness had endeared him to her, and much to his great surprise and joy he was the one she had smiled at. Immersed in a flood of emotions, resting his musket between his legs, the young sentry removed the small lace handkerchief from his tunic pocket. Its fragrant scent a reminder of the moment she had pressed it into his hand. The memory of the tears welling up in her eyes as he marched away down the narrow street. The sight of her waving after him until he was out of sight.

With the handkerchief still pressed to his nose, his thoughts consumed by the prospect of seeing her again, the young soldier's eyes suddenly widened in horror. Transfixed, he stared in disbelief at the terrifying apparition which had suddenly appeared before him. Then, before he had time to react, a hand was clamped over his half-open mouth, stifling the agonizing scream as the blade of a knife plunged into his heart. Confident that his life had ebbed away, pulling his knife from the soldier's chest Shingas gently lowered the sentry's body to the ground, and wiping the blood from its blade on the dead soldier's jacket he slipped the knife back into its sheaf. With the threat of discovery removed, silent as a shadow, he made his way into the camp. It didn't take him long to find Esther and the infant both fast asleep under a blanket not far from the flickering remains of the fire. Stooping down, Shingas carefully pulled aside a corner of the blanket and taking care not to wake him he scooped the infant up in his arms.

Esther wasn't sure what had awoken her. A premonition perhaps? Some sixth sense? Instinctively, she reached out her hand. Her child was gone. Horrified, she pulled herself upright with a scream welling up in her throat. Then she saw him sitting cross-legged opposite her, bathed in the soft glow of the dying fire with the infant cradled in his arms. Half afraid, half relieved for what seemed like eternity, unable to speak Esther stared across at him. Inscrutable as always, with the absence of war paint she detected a softness to his features, a gentleness mirrored in the way he was holding the child. Something she had glimpsed once before. It was clear that he had come for his child but if this were true, then why was he still here? She didn't have to wait long to receive her answer, as reaching out his arms Shingas handed her the sleeping infant. His jet-black eyes gazing into Esther's face as she took the baby into her arms, hugging him to her breast. With mother and child reunited, climbing to his feet Shingas slowly walked away. Disappearing like a phantom into the darkness beyond the fire.

For what seemed an age, wracked by indecision Esther sat staring into the darkness. Her mind awash with conflicting thoughts, each clamoring to be heard. Then, as though struck by a bolt of lightning, with unshakable clarity, she knew what she must do, and climbing to her feet, with the infant clutched in her arms she hurried after him.

In truth, she could have stayed. She could have allowed herself to be returned to the settlements with every chance that she would be claimed by Farmer Endicote. But what could she expect from him now except to be returned to a life of servitude? For with Saul dead there would be no need for her to become Adam's wife. But what concerned her most was the safety of her son, whose very presence would be a constant reminder to the bereaved farmer of those who had murdered his family. A memory so bitter she knew that eventually the hatred it engendered would consume him, and he would turn to her child for retribution. But no matter how compelling this scenario was, if she was truly honest the real reason for her decision to go with him, to turn her back on civilization, and return to a life amongst the Seneca was more personal.

Orphaned at the age of fifteen, when her father had finally succumbed to the grief which had been eating away at him since the loss of his wife and son, and put a pistol to his head, she had been condemned to a life of servitude. Passed from employer to employer like a piece of unwanted furniture. Her indenture eventually being purchased by Samuel Endicote. Living among the Seneca, and no longer seen by them as a captive, she had found freedom from this life of servitude. A freedom she was loathed to relinquish. She had also become part of a family. She had a child. She had a husband. Yes, it was true he was a savage, but she had glimpsed another side to his nature. She had seen this mask of inscrutability stripped away to reveal a person with a kind and loving heart. There was also her dear, darling Chantel who she missed desperately. A child who she had sworn to watch over. But for all this, the real act of persuasion, the true reason for her decision to return to a life among the Seneca came from knowing that he had feelings towards her. Feelings she never thought him capable of. A display of affection so profound that it had touched her heart. He could have taken his son and disappeared into the night never to be seen again. But instead, he had chosen to give him back to her. To allow her to choose their destiny, it was this act alone which now bound her to him. This single gesture which wedded her to him as surely as if a vicar had stood over them, and in the presence of God had pronounced them, husband and wife.

Silently, Shingas and Esther passed beside the young sentry slumped at the foot of the tree, the young girl's favor still gripped in his hand, and making their way towards the serried ranks of trees like moon-shadows they disappeared into the gloomy darkness of the forest.

Appendix

To ensure historical authenticity I have included extracts from the original documents held in the archives of the Pennsylvania Gazette at Harrisburg PA and the London Magazine for 1763. These include the letter from Captain Ecuyer to Captain Ourry and correspondence between Sir Jeffrey Amherst and Colonel Bouquet prior to and at the conclusion of the battle of Bushy Run.

Extracts of the speech by the Delaware chief Turtle Heart and Colonel Bouquet's response during the conference on the banks of the Muskingum River have been taken from Colonel Bouquet's official journals housed in the archives of the Pennsylvania Gazette.

This content was kindly provided by
Accessible Archives Inc. on-line databases.

About the author

Barry Cole was born in Yorkshire and after leaving the army he began contributing stories and articles to the monthly magazines of two Native American charities. With a love of film, he then studied for two years at the London Screenwriters Workshop. His first book, The Time Bandit was published in 2016, followed by a historical novel Shingas a few months later. His third book, The Conquistadors Horse was published in 2018 and has been optioned as a short film by Looking Window Pictures. The Letter, which was inspired by the Battle of Stalingrad was published in 2021. After living on a narrowboat for several years he has now returned to his roots in North Yorkshire. The idea for his fifth, A New Beginning came from a short screenplay written while studying at the Screenwriters Workshop which he now plans to rewrite as a feature. The principal character is named after the author's great-uncle, Albert Edward Clemens who died in August 1915 during the ill-fated Gallipoli campaign. Although the only thing they have in common is that both were soldiers his inclusion in the book is to celebrate the family's ancestral connection with one of America's greatest writers Samuel Langhorne Clemens, better known by his pen name Mark Twain. Set at the end of the Second World War, Hitler's Child is a whodunnit based partly on true events, exploring the mystery surrounding Hitler's death but with a twist in the tail.

Other books by Barry Cole

Suitable for Children as well:
The Time Bandit
The Conquistador's Horse

Historical Novels:
The Letter
A New Beginning
Hitler's Child

Your Satisfaction Is Our Goal!

Dear Reader,

We hope you enjoyed this book. Do you have any comments, criticism or ideas for books you want to read in the future? Please do not hesitate to contact us. We read every Email personally and answer it as soon as possible. Your opinion is of great value to us.

Contact us: info@ek2-publishing.com

You can help us to keep history alive by taking a moment's time to review this book online. Many positive reviews lead to more visibility for our books. A few words or a simple star review help our authors and our publishing company to increase our quality with every book published. Thank you for your support!

PS: In rare case scenarios a book might get damaged during shipment. If that should be the case, please do not hesitate to contact us and we will replace the book at no charge.

Your EK-2 Publishing Team

Our recommendation for you!

»Madame Moustache« takes you right to the California gold rush which lures thousands to the American West. Right in the middle of it all is a daring woman gambler who soon becomes a legend but also perishes because of it.
Eleanor Dumont breaks all the rules and is the first woman in Amerika to establish her own gambling saloon. But in a region full of danger and fleeting riches, a deadly drama unfolds. Based on true events, this book takes you back to the most exciting time of the pioneer days.

Available on all major platforms!

Published by EK-2 Publishing GmbH

Friedensstraße 12
47228 Duisburg - Germany
Register court: Duisburg - Germany
Company registration number: HRB 30321
CEO: Monika Münstermann

E-Mail: info@ek2-publishing.com
Website: www.ek2-publishing.com

Copyrights reserved.

Cover art: Mario Heyer
Author: Barry Cole
Editor: Manuela Schneider
Layout: Manuela Schneider

2nd. edition, February 2025

Made in United States
Troutdale, OR
03/29/2025